Oh My God! Are You Talking to Me?
(My Conversations with Jesus)

DEDICATION

Lovingly dedicated to the
Greater Glory of God (G.G.G.)

Out of my love for You, Jesus!

Peniel G.G.G.

Oh My God!

Are You Talking to Me?

(My Conversations with Jesus)

Book 1

Peniel G.G.G.

MI

METROPOLIS INK

ISBN 0-9580543-7-1

This novel is a work of fiction. All characters and events portrayed in this novel are either fictitious or are used fictitiously.

METROPOLIS INK
USA / Australia

web
www.metropolisink.com

email
inquiries@metropolisink.com

Just imagine... if you could speak casually with Jesus... if you could ask Him all of the questions that have puzzled (or haunted) you all of your life. This book is just that!

It is a transcript of a young man's casual conversations with Jesus.

That sounds extraordinary, doesn't it?

Well, you're right, it is... and then again, it isn't.

As Peniel (the young man who is speaking casually with Jesus) puts it, "What is so **extra-ordinary** about a Father talking to one of His loved children?"

This is the sort of simple reasoning that abounds in this unusual and enlightening book.

Please read it with an open mind—and perhaps you shall find what you really seek...

Signed,
God

Note at time of publishing.

It is now 2003, and I am finally able to commercially publish this book (which was written 18 years ago in 1985!).

If this book sells well, and I become "supposedly" famous, **PLEASE** don't let that stop you from contacting me if you want to talk! The reason Jesus had me to write this is to open the door so that I could talk to you, person to person, so that we can help you get back to that place you really want to be: happy, peaceful, and fulfilled! This is my MISSION in life! It is what I do! The books I write are merely to draw others to me, so that I might teach them (if they are sincere). Just get on the Internet and come here: www.mcwj.com

And no, I do NOT charge anything for teaching groups or individuals, or for any of my workshops and seminars. They are ALL free to any and all who wish to come; I give freely what Jesus has given to me freely!

Contents

Love 9
Man's Reason For Being 20
Why Man Chooses Wrongly 36
What Brings Man Good Fortune? 47
What Man Wants 57
Twelve Reasons Why Man Exists 69
Man's Single Largest Problem 80
Why Man Is Not His Natural Self 92
How To Be Your Natural Self 105
Some Sample Questions 111
Why Do We Hurt The Ones We Love? 113
What Man Fears Most 125
Joy And Suffering 137
Power 145
Perfection 152
Our Greatest Barrier To Truth 158
The Answer 174
Eliminating Pain And Suffering 184
Life Is For Enjoying 199
The Word 214
Love, One More Time! 225
Selected Love Passages 230
Peniel's Ode 237

Preface

Before you continue reading, please do as I ask of you here. Look around you and find some soil or dust. Place a few grains of it in your hand. Look intently at it. Study it for a couple of minutes. Once you have finished studying it, return to reading this preface.

If you really did get some and put it in your hand, congratulations—you have true personal integrity. If you did not really do it, please do it now. You will understand why afterwards.

Consider carefully what was just in your hand—what you have just experienced is a perfect reflection and mirroring of God's infinite power, knowledge, and beauty of creation…

… or else it is just dirt.

And this is as is my book. I hope that it does not turn out to be dirt for you!

Peniel G.G.G.

CHAPTER 1
Love

Me: God.

God: Yes, son.

I love You.

I know. I love you too.

I wish to love You more. I wish my love for You to be purer and stronger. How may this be done?

Learn of love.

Teach me about love.

I Myself **AM** love. Whenever you speak of love in the proper context, you speak of Me.

I have read that God is love.

Yes, and I meant it literally. Let Me give you some examples.

Okay.

Let us substitute several different statements in place of the word love and perhaps you will understand its true meaning. First, give Me an example using the word love in a sentence.

Okay. "I love Gail."

Now, substitute the phrase, feel and act the same way as God Himself does toward for the word love.

All right. I feel and act the same way as God Himself does toward Gail. Hmmm. You mean since You always feel and act out of love, because You are love, whenever I love I am just imitating what You would do?

In a way, yet it is not imitation. It is the natural way to feel and act—**with** love. Do this now: substitute <u>act naturally toward</u> for the word <u>love</u>.

All right. "I <u>act naturally toward</u> Gail." So love is just <u>acting</u> naturally?

Yes, only it's not an <u>act</u> in the sense of being phony. Remember, it is the natural way to feel and <u>treat</u> a person. The word <u>act</u> here may be difficult for you. Use the word <u>treat</u> instead.

So it's, "I <u>treat</u> Gail naturally."

Yes.

But what does that mean? What actions does love—or do You, being love—do?

See, already you begin to understand clearly. **I AM** love. Whatever love does, I do.

It pleases me to know that I am catching on. But explain what You—Love—does. If I know what love—God—does, then I may be more able to love properly; or as You put it, "be more able to feel and treat people the way God Himself would."

All right, here is something valuable for you to write down and pass on to others—too many have forgotten the activity of pure love that they knew as a child. **Love does two things:**

Love takes care of true needs.

Love gives pleasure to what it loves.

Simple, easy.

You mean that since You are love itself, **this is all that You do?**

Yes, I do two things only. These two things I have always done, for I have always been love itself. I will always do these in the future also, on into eternity. I do not <u>have</u> to do it—I <u>choose</u> to do it; for it is My nature to love—and I always do what comes naturally to Me.

So You, as God—as love—only take care of needs and give pleasure?

Yes, I love you. That is, I have the same feelings and actions as God Himself does toward you. Naturally, because I am your God. Stated another way, I act naturally toward you; I love you.

Does this mean that whenever I take care of another person's needs or give them pleasure that I am loving them?

Yes, so long as your motives are pure and the actions are appropriate.

You mean if I gave food to another person that needed it, but I only did it so that he would be indebted to me, that wouldn't be an act of love?

Correct, because your intention was selfish. Love is never selfish because **I am never selfish**.

Oh, I see! Whatever applies to You also applies to love—because You are love! And whatever applies to love also applies to You! **That's fantastic!**

Thank you. It pleases Me to see you really getting clear on this. I love you deeply, My son.

And I love You all that I can; yet, I know that I can love You better. Can I love You more?

Herein lies a dilemma and the biggest problem facing all of mankind since the dawn of man.

Oh, this sounds serious. What dilemma?

You cannot love Me as you now are.

How can You say that? I do love You! I would willingly die for You! You know that!

Yes, I do.

Well then, how can You say that man cannot love You?

Man can, only because I have provided a way. Hold on for a minute and calm yourself.

Now, what did I say love does?

You said love takes care of needs and gives pleasure.

Yes.

So?

So, what needs of Mine do you fulfill?

You don't need anything! You're God!

I know; do you understand?

Yes. So that means that I can't fulfill any of Your needs because You don't have any.

Right, and...?

Yes, but don't we give You pleasure?

Often you please Me; however, I am God—My joy and pleasure is infinite and complete at all times. Nothing can lower the amount of joy I have at any time. I am always completely full of joy.

But that's not fair. If You don't have any needs and we can't make You happier, then that means that we can't love You!

Not directly—not as you now are.

What do You mean by <u>as we now are</u>?

I mean in your fallen state. Before the Fall, man could love Me directly. We had open lines of love communion. Then, man cut himself off from My love. Man fell from My love.

I thought man fell from Your <u>grace</u>?

Yes. My love is grace. Whenever a person receives My grace, he receives My favor, and My favor is bestowed out of My love. It is an action of love. Doesn't grace take care of needs and give pleasure?

Yes.

Then it is an act of My love.

If we are fallen from Your love and can't love You directly as we now are, how can we fix this? Does this mean that we can't love You?

No. I have provided a way.

Teach me the way.

I AM. All that is—**I AM**. Whatever is powerful, noble, beautiful, and good—**I AM**. My presence, which is called life, is very close and intense inside of each person. Within each of you, **I AM**. Even though you may not be able to sense Me within your personality, which has been called soul and spirit, **I AM** closely and intensely present within you. Whatever good there is within you—**I AM**. For **I AM** Good. Outside of Me there is nothing that is good. So **I AM** the good and life within a person.

Wait a minute. You said that life is just Your presence, and soul and spirit really mean personality. Please explain these if You will. I want to be clear.

I will explain soon. Let us stay on the first subject for now. I realize that you are impatient to know everything.

Okay. I'll be more patient.

Let's see, You said that You are Good and You are the life within us.

Yes.

So that means that You are really present inside of each person.

Yes, and in so powerful and close a way that you may have trouble comprehending it. Let it be enough for now to accept that **I AM** within each person as the very core of their life and goodness.

Okay, I knew that before but I don't think I understood it quite as well as now.

I said this: "I will say to one person, 'I was hungry and you gave Me some food; I was thirsty and you gave Me a drink.'"

Yes, I remember the story. But You meant that they had done that thing to another person, right?

Right. Do you understand this?

Yeah, pretty clearly. But that means the bad as well as the good, doesn't it?

Yes.

You mean that every person I meet is really You in disguise?

(Chuckles.) No. Not in disguise, and they are not me. Yet, **I AM** fully present within that person. I have made you accountable for your motives and actions toward your neighbor in order to provide you with a way in which—once again—you may love Me.

Does this mean that if I am unkind or bad toward anyone that You're going to accuse me of doing that to You?

No. You have several misconceptions. Let Me clarify them one at a time.

Okay.

First, I would never accuse you of anything, even though I knew full well what you have done. I love you. Love does not make accusations! Experience this and know My love for all of you...

(Here, I was put into an experience of the woman about to be stoned for adultery and Jesus saved her [John 8:1-12.] I will not recount all of it here. The main point was that Jesus would not accuse her of her sins. He told her, "I accuse you of nothing.")

Wow! That's super! But does that mean that You don't care what we do?

No, I care very much; I just won't **accuse** you of your sins.

Does that mean that we're all home free? Without any accusation there isn't any trial, correct?

Correct. However you will be accused—just not by Me.

Let me guess who will accuse us—**Satan**.

Right. He is the accuser.

Okay, I see now.

Returning to the original subject: you will not be judged on whether you have treated every person you come in contact with as if they were Me.

Which ones will I have to treat as if they were You? I really need to understand this fully because a lot of things hinge on this, don't they?

Yes. The examples of how judgment will be made to determine a person's eternal place was based solely on how he had treated his neighbor.

Okay, I get the importance of this. Who is my neighbor that I must treat as if he were You?

(Here, I was put into an experience of the Good Samaritan story, and, as before, I will not recount it all here. Please look it up [Luke 10:25-37] before you continue reading because it is important that you understand what my neighbor meant.)

Do you see? I was asked the same question: Who is My neighbor that I must love as Myself? And this was My answer: Your neighbor is he who treats you with love.

So You mean that if a person takes care of me or gives me pleasure, then however I treat him, it will be as if I treated **YOU** that way.

Yes. You are obligated to treat Me with love whenever I come to you personally within another person.

But it's not really You; it's just some kind or helpful person.

No, **it is really Me**. Remember, whatever good is within a person is truly Me. Whenever a person loves another, it is the goodness within them doing the loving.

And You are that goodness.

Right. In essence, I love you through that person. I give him his life with My presence within him; I allow him to show Me (love) to you if he chooses to. The love that you have and express to another person both comes from Me and **IS** ME! Always remember: **I AM Love!**

So a person that is not loving me—that is, a person that is not willing to take care of my needs or give me any pleasure—is not revealing **You** (love) to me. So he's not **BE-ing** YOU to me.

That's correct. If he does not love you, then he is refusing to feel and act the same way as God Himself would toward you. Hence, he is not being Me (love) to you. I will not hold you accountable for your treatment of him as if he were Me, because I would not do the things he might do to you. I don't expect you to treat someone as if they were Me when they treat you with suspicion, anger, or hatred, for I would not treat you in that way. I love you.

I see. Dad?

Yes.

I love You more now, I think.

How?

I am clearer on what You wish for me to do. I will put forth great effort to love You more through loving my neighbor better.

This is good; it pleases Me that you are willing.

Will You teach me more?

Yes. What do you want to know?

Everything!

In time, I will teach you all that you wish to know, so long as you are willing to listen and it is good for you to learn. Be more specific for now. What do you want to learn now?

I wish to know the truth!

You know it already.

Do I? What is the truth?

I AM!

Oh, yeah. You are a lot of things. Well, if You are truth itself, and You are love, then truth is love?

Well, those are simply different aspects of Me.

How do You mean?

Whatever exists, exists in Me. I created it, I sustain it, and I move it. Except for personal beings—spiritual beings with free will—I guide, control, and work everything.

Okay.

There is a **TRUTH**. This simple TRUTH is the underlying principle behind all things. I was asked, "Why have You come?" and I answered that I came to testify to **THE TRUTH**. And I also said that anyone **COMMITTED** to the TRUTH, hears My voice.

You mean that anyone can really hear Your voice, as You have permitted me to hear You and talk with You?

Well, I didn't permit just you. I permit anyone to hear Me; the problem is that most people just won't listen or are not willing to pay the price for clear casual conversation with Me.

What is the price? Did I pay a price?

Yes, you became **COMMITTED** to the TRUTH.

I remember. Once I told myself that I was going to find the truth no matter what it took.

And what commitment did you make?

I said that no matter what the truth was, I would accept it and live my life by it. Even if it went completely against everything that I believed or held dear to myself, I would willingly turn all else loose for the truth.

This is the price. If you are willing to hear the truth, but you are not willing to accept it and live by it, then you are not yet fully committed to it.

I remember. And it was shortly after that when I developed the ability to hear You.

I am always willing to speak with My beloved children. Alas, many of them are unwilling or unable to hear Me clearly. I do strongly wish to speak to each of you.

Yeah, I guess You would be. You do love us so much.

Now, back to the TRUTH. There are many truths and only one TRUTH.

And You are that TRUTH?

Yes, and that truth, which is a particular aspect of Me, can be stated in a simplistic way in words.

You mean You can tell someone THE TRUTH? The Truth that underlies and determines all other truths?

Yes. Although, if it is stated without the proper foundation being laid for its comprehension, it will most likely be misunderstood.

Could I learn this TRUTH?

Yes—except not just yet.

Why not?

Because you still have a few essential misconceptions that would block your ability to fully understand it.

Such as?

Your false beliefs, your misconceptions, and your misperceptions.

Like not understanding what love really was?

Yes. What did you think love was?

Well, it's hard to explain. I guess I thought it was like a nice, warm feeling all over.

(Laughs.) So is a bath.

I thought it made you blind and do crazy things.

No! Love is not that way. I AM not that way. I don't make you blind or do crazy things. I assist you to see clearly and be mature if you allow Me to.

And I have misconceptions that are barriers to understanding TRUTH?

Yes. Tell Me what you think the TRUTH is?

God is love?

Sounds like a pat answer to Me. Come up with one of your own.

Well, the TRUTH has to deal with You. And I'll guess that it has to do with love, since You are love. I've got it! Man's reason for existence is to love and serve God! It's simple; it's the first commandment.

No. That's not the ultimate TRUTH, but it is a very close truth and I am pleased that you came up with that. Let's talk about man's reason for existing, for this, when clearly understood, will reveal the TRUTH.

You mean that man's reason for existence is the TRUTH?

Well, it's very similar.

So if You teach me why You created me—and all men—then I'll be able to understand THE TRUTH?

Yes. But we will have to lay some groundwork first to overcome some of your common misconceptions. After that you will be able to fully understand the TRUTH. It's not very complicated, yet it is very misunderstood.

Just like You and love, I'll bet. Okay, when?

Tomorrow. You need some sleep now.

I'll go to bed, but I don't think I'll be able to sleep. I'm too excited.

You got yourself excited. I'm here anytime you wish to talk with Me. I love you. I also know what's best for you. As you are, you shouldn't be in such a hurry to gulp down so much. Patience is also a virtue, along with holy zeal. Have some patience.

I'll try.

There is no such thing as "try" and you know it. Don't try—do it.

Yes, Father. I love You deeply; teach me to love You better.

I will, tomorrow. Go to bed now, and remember always: I love you!

CHAPTER 2
Man's Reason For Being

God: Well, how do you feel?

Me: I'm tired, but I feel good. I feel anxious about today. Might I learn the truth today as we talk?

If there are not too many barriers. I love you.

And I feel and act as God Himself does toward You also.

Do you realize that implies your love must be as Mine is—pure, intense, and non-judgmental?

Yes, I see that. It is not quite the same as what I believe many people mean when they say, "I love You." What is the difference?

My love is unreasonable.

I don't understand.

My love—pure love—is beyond reason. It is more noble and more powerful than reason. If you say, "I love you because..." and then you propose some reason why you love, that is not pure love. It is conditional love, tainted with human selfishness. True love—**ME**—is given without reason, unconditionally. I give Myself (love) to any who will receive Me. Yet I do not force Myself (love) on anyone. Each of you is free to accept Me (love) or reject Me (love).

So, whenever we accept love we are really accepting You?

Right. Anyone who loves purely is of God, for I Myself love through them. And, even if you know all things and have all power yet do not have Me (love), you have nothing of value! I am all that can be or is good. And what is the highest good?

You are—that is, **LOVE** is.

Very good. There is no higher or more noble action or spirit (personality) than **LOVE**. For none is above Me.

There, You said that spirit was really personality. Is that true?

In your modern terms, yes, but many words have changed their original meaning or have been perverted by misuse and misconceptions. I deal in pure concepts, so I choose those words out of your mind's vocabulary that are best suited to the intended meaning of My thoughts. Many words have been altered, such as ghost, spirit, and soul. Your soul is a spirit, which is a ghost. The Holy Spirit is My Ghost and My Soul.

Boy, I guess I don't understand. I thought that a ghost was some strange manifestation.

See? The Holy Ghost is no strange manifestation. Words such as these have had their meanings very confused.

Well, what can I do to clear it up?

For now, just substitute the most appropriate word in place of the problem word until you come to a fuller understanding.

You mean like You have been doing—like using the word personality in place of the words spirit or soul.

Yes. Spirit means what your modern word personality means, but the word spirit has taken on many different meanings. Exchange it a few times to see what I mean.

Okay, let's see. "God has a Holy Spirit," is really, "God has a Holy Personality." Great, I got that real clear! How about, "My soul will live forever and can never die," is really, "My personality will live forever and can never die." Okay, I got that too; this will be very useful!

It pleases Me to make you happy.

Okay, what is the **TRUTH**?

You tell Me.

I think it has to do with You (love), truth, and man. By the way, is there a substitute for the word man? I think it is one of those very misused words.

Certainly: Children of God, Sons and Daughters of God, Children (Sons and Daughters) of Love. Gods, Mini-gods.

You're kidding, right?

No. Man is divine. Man is immortal. Man is infinite. Man is more powerful than all of nature and the universe combined.

How can that be?

Because man can do what nothing or no one else (except I) can do—the highest good and most noble activity of all.

Which is?

Man can **BE** God. Man has total free will and he can choose to be anything he wants. He can be low, vile, evil, and worldly, or he can be noble, loving, benevolent, and divine. He can alter his actions, personality—even his very being—at will. He is totally free to do, be, act, choose, and feel any way he chooses at any and all times. Man has infinite free will and choice—just like Me. Therefore, man may be as God—if he chooses to utilize fully his power.

You mean no one can force me in anything?

Right. You may do a thing because you are afraid of the possible consequences, yet the decision was solely yours to make. Others may only *influence* your decisions, not determine them. Already I've told you how rare and valuable you are.

Yes, I remember. You have given us a mighty set of tools to use.

Yes, your physical body is a great accomplishment of Mine, yet it doesn't even start to compare with your personality.

You mean my immortal soul, right?

Right. And now that you understand that, let's return to the Truth. What is man's reason for being? Why are you here?

Well, I thought it was to love and serve You—like the first commandment.

That is part of it, yet it is not the primary reason why I created you.

Well, is it to love our neighbor and thereby love You?

No.

I give up. Will You explain it to me now?

Yes. Let Me ask you some leading questions and allow you to discover the TRUTH for yourself. This will help you to understand it more clearly and be able to teach it to others.

Fine.

What is man?

A Son or Daughter of You (Love, God).

Good. What am I?

The Perfect Loving Father.

Marvelous. Remember this first point! We shall have to keep returning to the basics to understand simplicity. So who am I?

Now. What about the TRUTH?

More questions first. Am I fair?

Yes, completely.

Am I just?

Yes.

Am I reasonable in actions?

Yes—except in loving, because that's unreasonable.

True. Yet even though it's not reasonable, you now know what love does for you when you receive it?

Sure.

Now let's talk some about the primary reason why man exists. I am a loving Father. Do you know what it is like to be a loving father?

Yes. You sent our daughter Summer to us so that we could be loving parents.

Do you love Summer?

Yes.

And are you her father?

Her <u>human</u> father. You are her true Father.

Right. Now I'll let you explain to Me why a loving father has a child; this will teach you why I have all of you.

Why did you choose to have Summer?

Because we wanted a child.

Why? Isn't it difficult, a lot of responsibility, restricting to your freedom, and many other negative things?

Yes, but it has more overpowering positive things about it.

Such as?

Well, like I get to be a dad.

What does that mean?

Having someone to love.

You had Gail, your wife. Why not love her?

I did love her, and I wanted to love a child too.

Wouldn't you have to divide your love between them and then each of them would receive less?

No. You never run out of love; the more you give, the more you have to give.

Okay, then why not find a friend and love them?

It's just not the same.

Why? What's the difference between loving a child and loving a friend?

They're not related to me.

So?

They're not mine.

Neither is a child. They don't belong to their parents like a car or a stereo, they belong to themselves!

I know. I didn't mean it like that. I mean that Summer is made out of me—she's a part of me. She is half me.

And how does that make you feel?

Good. Extremely **goooood**!

And that is **GOD!** God is short for Goooood! It's a title, like king or Perfect Loving Father—that's **WHAT** I am, not who I am.

I get it, by having Summer—and Summer being part of me, and through my loving her—I AM GOOOOOD; I BECOME **GOD**!

At least to Summer you are God. Both you and Gail have been made co-Gods (mini-Gods) for Summer. I Myself have made it this way.

So was it this way for You? I mean does it apply to You like You make it apply for us?

Exactly. There's nothing deep or mysterious about the TRUTH. It's very simple; although when you fully grasp it, it might stun you!

Well, I'm still eager to find it out. What is it—why are we here, mainly?

You tell Me. Why did you two have Summer?

Because we wanted to love her; that is, we wanted to take care of her needs and give her pleasure. We wanted to be Love (God) FOR her.

Didn't you want her to serve you?

Of course not. I'm fully grown; I don't need anyone to…

(Strange silence)

What?

I got it!

Tell Me what you got.

THE TRUTH! Why You made me. Man, that's so wild. It's almost the exact opposite of what we believe.

Say it!

You created me so that **YOU COULD SERVE ME!** Love's action is service. I had Summer to give her pleasure and take care of her needs for her, and that is good—and that makes me feel goooood—and that makes me God. AND THAT IS MY FULFILLMENT—TO BE AS YOU ARE! You made us so that You could be our God; that is, so that You could be good to us and serve us and make us happy! That means that THE TRUTH IS:

GOD IS THE SERVANT OF MAN! YOU MADE US SO THAT YOU COULD LOVE US, AND THIS MAKES YOU OUR GOD!

Very good. I didn't create man only to serve or love Me. I made you so that I could love you; and, if you were willing to return love to Me then I would accept it. I made you to love. **I loved you first!**

But You are God. You are much greater than we!

Which only means that I love more and more purely.

I get it; and love **serves**. That means that Your fulfillment is to love us.

Yes. It is what makes Me God (Goooood) to you. I would still be your creator if I didn't love you, yet you would not accept Me as **God** (goooood) to you. I am the great king bowing down to wash the feet of his servants. **Did you not know... THIS IS LOVE!**

So man's primary reason to exist is to allow You to love us—that is, to allow You to take care of our needs and give us pleasure!

Correct.

Well, it's all mixed up down here. If I asked a hundred people on the street why they thought God made us, ninety of them would say to love and serve God, eight would say that they didn't know, and the other two would tell me to mind my own business! I don't know anyone that realizes this TRUTH. We think that we are supposed to serve and love You.

And how would you do that? Can Summer serve your needs?

Not very well. I don't want or expect her to serve me, I want to serve her. I love her! All I want is to take care of her and give her joy.

Okay, let's switch the roles so that you'll understand it better. You will be Me and Summer will be mankind.

All right.

Let's say Summer turns ten years old, and one of her friends convinces her that what you really want is for her to serve you; that this is why you created her.

Well, I'd just tell her that that's not true. I can serve myself. I want to serve her instead—that's why I really made her.

Hold on. She is fallen from your love, remember? She can't hear you or won't listen.

Well, then I'd demonstrate it for her.

She doesn't accept reason or logic. She says, "Dad, I'm ten years old now and I've been sponging off of you long enough. I'm going to go to work and serve you and pay you back for everything you have done for me."

That's crazy! I don't want her to leave me. I don't need her to serve me. She can't do anything better for me than I can do for myself. I only want for her to be with me and accept my love!

She is firmly convinced otherwise. If someone were to tell her, "Summer, your father doesn't want you to serve him; he wants to serve you!" she'd tell them that they were crazy—the very idea, God serving man—it's preposterous, they would all say.

I see, and since it's so difficult to communicate with us, Your hands are pretty much tied. We have a hard time getting this TRUTH.

Okay, she's grown and has kids of her own. What will she tell them about what you want from them?

She'll tell them that God wants them to serve Him. And they'll teach it to their kids—and so on for generations.

And what did your earthly father tell you was the reason that God created you?

To serve and love God.

I do want you all to love Me and serve Me in the way I choose for you to; yet, this is secondary. I want more for you to willingly **receive** My love for you! Your main reason for being is **to receive My love—** that is, to receive **ME**. Nothing is more important. This is My will and wish above all other things: to love you. I showed this clearly in the way I chose to save mankind through willing laying down My own mortal life in an agonizing and unjust death. I could have done it in other ways, but I chose to do it that way to show all of you just how much I love you.

My God—I never really understood all this before! I knew, but I didn't understand just how much You loved us.

You know and understand how much you love Summer and what you would be willing to do for her; this applies to Me also for I am a loving Father to all of you. And I will love you all that you will let Me, just like you would love Summer. Let Summer and her relationship with you be the model for our relationship.

Okay.

When I love you a great deal, do you think you will feel unworthy of it?

I think so. I think I may feel that I don't deserve it and shouldn't accept it.

And if you threw Summer a surprise party just because you love her and bought her a wonderful gift, and she refused to accept it because she feels undeserving, how will this make you feel?

Sad. I know that she doesn't deserve it—she couldn't. No one said anything about deserving. I did it because I wanted to and I love her! I want to give her pleasure and joy. Oh man! I get it!

Now do you see how I get treated?

Yes—I have done that to You many times myself. I have refused Your love and gifts because I felt that I didn't deserve them.

How would you want Summer to respond when you gave her something extravagant and undeserved?

I would like her to accept it. Absolutely no words such as, "You shouldn't have," or, "I can't accept it." I want her instead to say, "Oh, how wonderful. A surprise party for me! How marvelous! Dad, you're so wonderful and I love you very deeply. Let's eat the cake and open the presents!"

And how would that make you feel if she accepted it with easy grace and excited joy?

Fulfilled. Like I intended to feel—why I did it in the first place! I'd feel **Goooood**. I'd be her God again!

Oh, you're getting very clear on this subject! Loving, purely, makes you God! And when you refuse to let Me love you...

I got it. I refuse to let You BE GOD (loving) to me! I get it—it's so simple. You are our God only when we let You be Goooood to us. WE make You our God when we let You love us!

Yes, yet how many people let Me be God to them or are even aware of this peculiar relationship?

I don't think there are very many. It should be all of them.

And now I will state THE ULTIMATE TRUTH that underlies and creates all other truths—this is why I came to the earth and what I continually demonstrated with My words, life, and actions...

I AM GOOOOOD (GOD) AND I LOVE YOU.

I see it clearly now. I also see that if You had just come right out and told me that the truth was that God loves me, I would have said, "Oh, sure, I knew that," but I wouldn't have grasped what it really meant—all that it means. I still don't think that I will ever fully grasp all that it means!

Yes, but you do understand it much better already, don't you?

Yes. But most of us already have our minds made up about You and love and what the truth is and what it means that God loves us and just about everything else that is important or essential in life.

I think that we have made many errors and are mistaken about what a lot of these truths really mean.

Yes, to simply tell most people the simple truth, such as "God loves you!" does them little good because they already think they know what that should mean.

So how do I assist them to really grasp and understand these simple truths that are so misunderstood?

You either have to assist them to overcome their misperceptions first, and then do a lot of redefining and explaining and clarifying later, or something much simpler.

What is that?

Do what I Myself did. Demonstrate it to them with the example of your life. If you show them that you love them and that you are Goooood then they might pick up on it. They may even be willing to listen sincerely to your guidance and teachings, and this way you can best assist them.

I see.

You know what?

What?

I LOVE YOU!

Finally, I think I understand You.

Good. Will you let Me love you more, as is My wish?

Yes. Will You help me and teach me to better love You in return?

(Laughs.)

What's so funny?

You tell Me—what would you do if Summer asked you if you would be willing to teach her to receive your love better?

(Laughs.) I guess I'd laugh, because it's a silly question; of course I would be willing—I love her!

(Laughs again.)

Okay, that's one of my misperceptions— that sometimes God might not be willing to help me do something good.

And to get rid of a misperception you must first identify it, and then reason it through.

Well, I know that You are willing to assist me because You love me. So where did I come up with that particular misconception? Why do we sometimes think things about You that aren't true?

A child's mind is a wonderful thing. However, their emotional ability far exceeds their reasoning capacity for many years. You know how easy it is to get a child to believe some fantasy. They are very trusting and swayed easily.

Okay, but how do we get the misperception?

From God.

Surely not; You wouldn't lead us astray.

No I wouldn't; but the God of children might.

Oh, yeah. My parents were my perceived Gods before I learned about You. I remember when I was young how I thought my parents were perfect and could do no wrong. I guess I did think they were God.

As do most all children. There's nothing wrong with this conception as long as the parents are very good and know the truth.

Why is that?

Whatever a parent teaches a child through example and action, a child will accept as true. This is because the child believes his parents are Goooood and couldn't make any mistakes.

I see. The child wouldn't question or analyze the reasonableness of their parent's examples. Why should they? It was their God that taught it to them.

Right. And so they believe that is the way God is—the way their parents were. And what do you suppose they do when they find out about Me—the real God?

They project their earlier beliefs about God (gotten from their parents when viewed as God) on You. That's why I thought that You might not be willing to help me—because there were times when my earthly father was unwilling to help me with something. I thought he was God, and therefore I thought that God was like that. I guess I didn't understand that he was just human and sometimes made errors in judgment just like everyone. And when I did finally learn about You, personally, I carried over many of my earlier perceptions about what God was like that were based on my earthly parents' actions. I guess I have many misperceptions to overcome about You.

And do you understand that this is the way it is for most of you?

Yes, I have seen it in many people's belief systems. I just didn't understand how people got such strange ideas about You before.

And were your beliefs correct?

Many of them weren't.

Now, what do you think determines how many and how serious the misperceptions a person has about Me and the truth?

It depends on how close your parents act compared to the way God would act. If both your parents were very good, loving, perfect people then you would think God is like that and you'd be correct. But if your parents were very bad, evil, hateful, and uncaring people then you'd mistakenly believe that God was like that.

That's basically it. The better your parents are, the less serious your misperceptions about Me and truth will be.

Thank God my parents were pretty good people.

You're welcome! (Chuckles)

I guess that means that I won't have too many misperceptions about You.

No, you're already pretty clear. And remember, we've been talking for several years now. Even recounting some of our earlier conversations like we are doing here is helpful to you. You've come to know Me pretty well. What do you think of Me?

You're the greatest. You're loving, good, caring, simple, and humble—and a lot of fun!

And what about you?

Well, I'm not You yet, but I am working on it.

Yes. You do realize of course that all you are really doing is becoming yourself. The person who was given the name Mark Anthony Johnson by his parents at birth is becoming Peniel (his true name that I Myself gave him) through My guidance. You are in the process of coming back to yourself. You, like all of My children, were made in My image; that means when you become your true self, it is a mirroring of Me. You put on Christ and become Christ-like. It isn't an act or an imitation—it is just that your being your natural self closely resembles Me.

That's marvelous! I have much to look forward to.

Now, to become more like Me—your true self—what must you do?

Understand You, love, truth, myself, and everything better.

Okay, then what?

Do what comes naturally to me.

And what would that be?

The same things as You do.

Which is?

Love purely.

And what would you love?

I'd love You first, but I wouldn't cut You off from loving me.

And?

I'd love myself.

And?

I'd love my wife.

And?

I'd love my neighbor.

And?

I'd love nature.

And?

My God—You sure do love a lot! I could never find the time to love all this!

Love doesn't need time. You don't have to find time to love. Love itself will provide you with time if you are sincerely willing to love more. Is there another false belief floating around in your mind?

I guess so—that I don't have the time to love all.

Who taught you that?

God, my earthly father. Sometimes he wouldn't find the time to love me or others. He could have—but he chose not to. And then he used the excuse that he COULDN'T find the time. I guess I picked it up from him. Sometimes he didn't have the time to love me when I really needed it and I remember how hurt I was. Oh, God, I do that to Summer sometimes!

Then don't! Choose to love rather than to ignore! Make the time! If you are sincere in your attempts then I Myself will assist you and make the time for you. All you have to do is ask.

I'm getting something else.

What?

You're showing me that because You love me, You will do anything good for me—if I only ask You!

Wouldn't any loving father do the same for his loved children?

Yes, but I guess we forget this often. You are showing me another of the main principles?

Yes. What is it?

All things work for the good of him that loves God purely.

Right. Now you have two simple and powerful principles to guide your life by—if you choose to.

If I remember these two and really apply them to my life, my life will become much richer than it is now!

And this would please Me very much.

Just think: what God really wants most is to take good care of me and give me all the joy that I will accept—and God has so much power! My life will have no more worry and be filled with joy when I fully accept and apply these principles.

I ask you and anyone that will later read this work the most important question of your life concerning just this...

WHEN? WHEN WILL YOU ACCEPT ME??

I for one accept You now, sweet Jesus. Please come into my life and take care of all my needs and give me all the pleasure that You will. I willingly accept You and Your love!

Thank you, my darling child. Prepare yourself, for I am about to change you and fill your life full of every good and joy! I love you, Peniel!

And I love You, Father.

CHAPTER 3
Why Man Chooses Wrongly

Me: Well, how are You today?

God: Perfect. I'm always perfect and never felt better.

Oh, yeah. I keep forgetting. I keep assuming that You're like us.

Let's talk about that.

Okay. You see, You've helped me to see clearly what a real, down-to-earth person You are; I sometimes view You as human.

I am human, just as you are divine.

No, humans can be bad and do evil. You can't.

Yes I can.

When were You ever bad or when did You ever do anything wrong?

Never.

So there You are—<u>You're not human</u>.

What do you think <u>human</u> means? What is a human being?

A child of God that can love, can choose, and can reason.

Very good—you remember our earlier conversations well. And where in that description does it say that a human being must do wrong?

Where it says <u>can choose</u>. That means we are free to choose to be bad or do evil if we wish to.

And do I have this power also, or did mankind create it? Is there anything that I cannot do?

No.

Then do I have the power and ability to do wrong or be bad?

Yeah, I guess You do.

I certainly can.

But You don't. How is that?

I choose not to; yet, I have the power. Satan did not create or invent evil. All power is contained within Me.

You mean there's evil within You?

Is there such a thing as evil?

I believe so.

And is it in existence?

Yes, if it is a real thing.

Is there anything that exists that I did not create or do not possess within Myself?

No.

Well, what have you answered to your own question?

You do have the capability to sin. It's one of Your powers. You simply choose not to ever sin or be bad because it's not part of what comes naturally to You. But You **can** sin if You choose to!

Does this shake you?

It kinda startles me. God can sin.

Ask this instead: "**Will** God ever sin"?

No. You wouldn't.

Then it doesn't change your opinion about Me?

No. I think I respect and admire You more now.

Why?

Because it's not fixed; You can sin—just like us. You have to choose not to just like we do, and, You always choose the right thing! It must feel great to have that much power.

It does. How does it feel to be divine?

Why ask me? You're the divine one.

And you're not? Don't you have the power to always choose good if you want to—just like Me?

Yes, I do.

Every time?

Yes, otherwise I would be forced to do something evil and that isn't fair—You wouldn't allow it.

Certainly not. So you can choose good, right, and correct every time, just like Me—if that's your choice?

Yes, I have that power—You gave it to me.

So how does it feel to be divine and have that much power?

Super, but when I choose to be bad or do evil it feels awful.

So, don't do it. Choose correctly instead.

But sometimes I can't help myself!

Aha! Here's another false belief that I have drawn out into the open. CAN you help yourself?

Well, yes, I guess I could. I could always ask You for help before I choose wrongly, and, in that way at least, I can always get help.

So why don't you?

I get it! I choose not to. The truth is, sometimes I won't help myself! I CAN—I just choose not to.

Congratulations, another mistaken belief is overcome.

But why don't I always help myself?

You don't always want to.

But I do! I want to always do what is "good" and never offend or hurt You or refuse Your love! I really want to do the right thing!

EXCEPT... when you choose to do otherwise.

But that's stupid! Why do I so often choose to be bad over good?

Why indeed? You have the power to choose any way you wish.

Yeah, I have the power, because like You, I'm divine in nature by my own choice. You have given me the power and I have chosen to use it; but I still choose evil oftentimes. Granted, they're not what most people would consider big sins, but You have already shown me how every offense against Your love is a terrible thing because of Your goodness and purity. Whenever I sin against You—even just a small offense in man's eyes—it is a terrible crime and I have been informed of this.

Why do I still do the things that I don't want to do and why don't I even ask for Your willing help in my moments of temptation? I'll bet it's tied up with my false beliefs, just like all my other problems and barriers that stand between me and my own perfection, isn't it?

Yes, you learn quickly!

So, what false beliefs would make—I mean <u>cause</u>—me to choose evil? I know that it will hurt You, hurt me, and only do harm. I know that when I do these things it will be just like always; it will do no good and cause me a lot of suffering and guilt.

So, why?

One reason—I used to believe, until You just showed me the truth—is that I thought I had NO CHOICE.

Very good. And now you know that this isn't true. Will you ever sin again or do any evil or choose wrongly?

I hope not, but I'm sure I will.

Okay. Let's help you in this area by discovering the truth about the situation as it really is.

Please. If it can assist me on my path to perfection, I'll do anything.

Good. Now, why do you think that you will sin again? What will cause or sway you to do it?

More false beliefs, I guess.

Such as?

I don't know.

Do you really not know?

Well, I probably do know; I just can't think of it right now.

You can't?

I see, another false belief. I can think of it, I'm just choosing not to!

Clever. Do you see how you do this to yourself?

Yeah, I keep telling myself that I can't do such-and-such, and then I accept and believe that, and then I choose not to do it because I wrongly believe that I have no choice about it.

Right. You devalue yourself. You limit your own power and choices by accepting a false belief.

Does that mean that if I get rid of these false beliefs that I will not sin anymore or do any evil?

No. You'll still be free to choose to do good or evil just as you are now; however, you won't be operating from automatic and self-defeating beliefs as you now are. You WILL have a choice and you will know it!

You mean that some of my wrong choices right now stem from automatic behavior?

Yes. You simply don't choose because you have made yourself believe that you have no choice. Some of your bad habits or sinful acts become habitual. Man is a creature of habits when he matures physically.

I get that. Now, how may I use this to my advantage?

Simple: form good, holy habits of love to replace your bad, evil habits of restriction.

Okay, I'll do it.

Now let's talk more about false beliefs.

Good. This seems to be our big problem area.

Once you overcome almost all of your false beliefs, will you still be able to choose evil or sin?

Yes. I will still have that power; but I probably won't choose it nearly as often as I do now.

Why not?

Because, like You said, now a lot of my wrong choices stem from automatic behavior because of these false beliefs. When the false beliefs are mostly gone, I will be able to overcome the automatic behavior.

Okay. Will you ever do evil again?

I hope not; but I probably will. There's more for me to do than just overcoming the false beliefs.

Such as?

Well, if I didn't stop and think about it, I might do evil just out of habit. Now, when I choose to do what's wrong, I choose to because I mistakenly believe that this evil is really good for me. I NEVER choose to do anything that I really believe is not good for me.

What about when you fast or pray, or willingly suffer for Me because I ask you to?

I do that because I believe it is in my best interest. I realize that serving You in the way You wish me to is in my ultimate best interest.

Very good; and it is in your best interest. However, you serve Me best—as we discussed earlier—by becoming your true self first and then doing what comes naturally to you and following My instructions.

Right.

And everything I choose to do is in My best interests also.

But You always choose to do the right thing!

I have no false beliefs to blind Me from the right choice, I have no bad or evil habits, I don't operate from automatic behavior, and I know what is true and good, always. I don't deceive Myself, I accept all of My choices and full responsibility for them, and I have complete confidence in My maturity and integrity. How could I go wrong?

And if I was like that, could I be as good as You?

You would have the power and choice, so yes.

So I need to overcome my false beliefs, get rid of my bad habits and form good ones, stop operating from automatic behavior, and learn what is true and good. I also need to stop deceiving myself, accept my choices and responsibility for them, and develop complete self-confidence in my maturity and integrity. That's a tall order!

Not really. It's only natural for you. All you have to do is become your true self—Peniel already has all these qualities! Remember, he's mirroring Me because he was made in My image.

It seems like a lot.

It's a long way back to Georgia from Las Vegas, yet you could walk there if you took it one step at a time, moving forward not backward, and going in the right direction—slowly, steadily, surely, patiently. Don't stop yourself, don't turn back, and don't give up. You'll make it all the way.

Okay, I get that. One step at a time. But which way, which step first, what pace? If I am going to travel from Mark to Peniel and I don't know the way, I will need a guide!

I will walk beside you every step of the way, guiding you, teaching you, assisting you, encouraging you, loving you, and carrying you if you <u>cannot</u> go any further on your own.

Will there be many barriers?

Many.

How large will the barriers be?

Mountains.

How shall I cross them?

With Me. Together, what is there that we cannot do?

Nothing, as long as You are with me.

I am with you always—I love you.

I love You, too.

Then follow Me. Let Me lead you back home.

Where is my home?

Home is where you are—the real you, not the you that you show to others.

And where is the real me?

Here with Me!

Can I travel from where I am to where I AM?

Yes.

Is it far?

As far as you make it!

Do I have to go?

No. As always, you may choose as you like.

What if I don't follow You now?

By your own choice, you would leave Me. For I am traveling to where the real you is. Walk with Me if you choose; we will talk along the way and I will love you. I will show you many wonderful things and teach many of My children through you, if you follow Me. This is why I have created you. This is My wish for you: walk with Me, I offer you a valuable gift—YOURSELF.

I will walk with You—lead me where You will. I know that if I am with You and I fall, You will help me back up and say nothing about my slip. If we go high, then that is the way we should go. If we descend low, then that is where we should go. Wherever You lead me will be the best route—for I know well enough to trust You with my life.

I love You, and if my love is not pure, I will purify it. And if I do not know how to purify it, teach me. And if You cannot teach me, then purify my love for me, for this is my wish. And I know that after receiving Your love for me, to love You perfectly is my most noble destiny and purpose.

In my earlier quest for knowledge I read many, many books and learned many facts until I had amassed a great pile of knowledge, which I now count as dirt. Nothing in my life is important, save loving You only. And if a thing does not assist me to love You more purely or assist one of my willing and sincere brothers to love You better, then I count it as nothing—and as nothing I shall treat it. Whatever is not You is nothing and I see it as nothing. All of the vain knowledge of men is as a mountain of dirt and I wish no part of it. For it has previously hindered me from my true destiny: being in a good loving relationship with You. Only loving You and following You has ever given my life any fulfillment and direction.

I willingly offer You my body, mind, personality, and life; guide and use me as You will—I AM YOURS. Let Your wish be my will now and forever. I live for You only; come and make Your abode in me if it be Your desire. Let us be one together for all eternity. I love You and want nothing but You forever. I LOVE YOU—TEACH ME TO LOVE YOU MORE PERFECTLY!

I am deeply moved by your love of Me. And now I again accept your loving offer, for I love you. I have created you to love you and I choose to walk with you and lead you back to yourself, your innocence and purity. I will show you your true worth and allow you to accept back your integrity. I will speak with you and teach you of Me and yourself. You will not fall for I will hold you tightly, unless you push Me away. I will take you high, for it is good for your spirit to soar when it is time. I will take you low, so that you can recognize the baseness and evil of your old self that still lurks within you. I will lead you and always will I assist you to choose what is best, if you will only ask Me. For I do love you, and nothing deceives Me.

I will teach you to love Me and your fellow man and all things with a pure and perfect love as My love is. Then I will make My abode with you and My Father will come with Me. We shall live together within your soul. And where We are, there heaven is.

So We shall bring heaven itself to you and you shall reside there as best a mortal man may. As you feel towards your children, with even your love still not perfected, I feel towards you—except with perfect intensity, purity of intention, and strength of will.

Yet, My Father and I would never force ourselves upon you; you will have to ask Us to make Our home within you when the time is right. And We cannot make Our abode within you until you are perfect in spirit, for We will not abide where the beasts of evil also dwell. Once you drive away all evil from your personality and prove your sincerity in safeguarding yourself from evil and the occasions of sin, then We will invite you to allow Us into your heart, mind, and very self. And when We do make Our house with you, We shall give you every grace and good that is destined for you. Together we have a world that we can change for the better, if that be our choice. Yet, we will start with you.

All this will come to pass if you choose to follow Me and love Me. And he who loves Me will keep My commandment to you: Love God perfectly, and love your neighbor as yourself. I appreciate the value and worth of your sacrifice and you shall be rewarded handsomely for your sincere love and willingness. You may take back the gifts I gave you of your own life and free will at any time, for I always offer them back to you. If you choose as I desire for you to, and leave these precious clothes in My care for awhile, then I will cleanse them of their filth, mend their tears, brighten their colors, and sharpen their lines. I shall make you a new man, your true self, a perfect being, a real man among mere men. You will be a beautiful loving creation reflecting My very self with actions and motives pure as the first snow. You will have power and authority over all that you should be over. You will be fully My son, and I am a powerful King. You shall be My beloved Prince and I shall be proud of you!

And by your example others may be moved to be better men also. And you shall do great important work just by being your true self. Many are not yet fully committed to the truth, so as yet many will not hear Me like you do. You will hear Me and I shall speak to others through you. This is also My will for you, and I have destined it for you from your very creation. For I love you, as I love all My children; yet you are more willing to receive My love and return My love and follow Me. The choice of all this is now, and always shall be, yours alone.

You may follow Me and take all that I have destined for you, or you may reject Me and go your own way. I may lay My own cross upon your shoulders to carry for a while. And if I do, remember that all that I do to you is in your best interests and done out of My love for you. I love you, and the choice is all yours!

Follow Me, Peniel.

I will follow You. I offer You all things, for all good, always and all ways. Guide and love me.

CHAPTER 4

What Brings Man Good Fortune?

God: Tell Me, what have you learned?

Me: I have learned two great principles so far: One, God Loves Us, and two, all things work for the good of those who love the Lord purely.

Very good. Can you sum up what you have learned?

Yes. I should love my neighbor as myself, for he who is my neighbor loves me, and he who loves me is God to me, and as God I should treat him—with sincere and pure love.

Very good. Let's talk more about the second principle that you have learned: all things work for the good of those who love the Lord. What do you think about this?

I'm sure it must be true.

Why?

Three reasons: one, my own personal experience will testify to this fact; two, it is logical and reasonable; and three, You said it was so.

Let's expand upon it and learn more about it.

Sure.

How do I treat those who love Me purely?

With love.

And what does love do?

Takes care of true needs and gives all the pleasure that will be received.

And what is the best state for a man to be in?

The natural state; the state of being his natural self. Then, he will think, act, feel, and be natural. This is the best state for a person to be in—perfection.

You remember well. And when a man is himself, what results come in his life?

He receives into his life three things more valuable than all earthly possessions: success, well-being, and good fortune. Together these three are called **Nirvana**.

And what is a success?

A person who possesses all that he should in the proper amounts.

And what is well-being?

To be fulfilled and have all good and positive attitudes, feelings, health, and emotions.

And what is good fortune?

When most of the things that a man is not free to choose for himself seem to line up in his favor; such as a book that just happens to cover the answer to a question that he was looking for is given to him by a friend. Nature itself seems to favor you and your service and pleasure, such as it raining when your crops need water and it staying dry when you go on a picnic even though they predicted rain. Most people call this good luck.

Fine. And good fortune is what we shall talk about first.

Okay.

How is your luck?

You know that I know there is no such thing as **luck**.

Chance?

No such thing—You don't roll dice!

Are you fortunate? Do you have good fortune?

Yes, very much so. Ever since I have really loved You purely, all things have worked for my advantage and pleasure.

And how have you felt?

Fulfilled, peaceful, joyous!

Why?

Because either You have given me these feelings of Your own choice, because You wished to show me that You love me, or else they are the natural result of my nearing my <u>natural</u> self.

And does it matter which way it happens?

No. It only matters that it happens and that it is good.

Why would I give a person this fulfilled feeling you say you felt?

To tell him that he is finally on the right track in life.

And why do you think more people do not feel fulfilled?

Because most of them are going in the wrong direction in life. You certainly wouldn't reward a person with those feelings if he were not doing what You really wished him to do in life; that would encourage him in the wrong way.

Do I wish for all of My children to have fulfillment?

Yes.

Then why do so few have it?

Few are willing to follow their true destined path.

If they were willing to do as I ask of them, would they then receive good fortune?

Yes, good fortune is just another way of saying that a person has **God's favor**. It means that You favor them; and You favor those who do Your will. And Your will is for them to allow You to love them and to love You through loving themselves and their neighbor. Those You favor receive what we call <u>good fortune</u>.

Very good. You remember what I have taught you.

Why don't more people realize this? It seems very simple and logical.

You remember Peniel's Ode, *The Fool In The Cave?* (See appendix.)

Of course. It is an analogy of my life.

Why is Peniel different from the others?

He has almost no misperceptions. He sees things clearly.

This is why. Most people have so many misperceptions they can't even understand the basic questions they should be asking—much less the answers.

Now let's talk about <u>destiny</u>.

Okay.

Who chose your parents for you?

You did.

Who chose when in time you would live?

You did.

And who decided what particular talents, skills, and abilities you would have as part of your <u>natural</u> self?

You.

And who chooses the weather for you for a particular day?

You.

And who chose the way you would look?

You.

And who chooses everything that is beyond your own personal choice or influence?

Sometimes You, sometimes other people. Such as, my parents chose what beliefs I would be taught.

True. And can I influence the choice of others if I wish to?

Yes, You can exert great influence; but You would rarely force anyone.

And if I really wished for you to go to a certain school, or read a certain book, or meet a certain person?

Yes, You have a great deal of influence if You choose to take matters into Your own hands.

And if I desired for you to have a certain career?

Yes, You could arrange and greatly influence anything that You put Your mind to—few people doubt that You have great power.

So if I wanted certain things for you, could I arrange it?

Yes, anything at all. So long as You didn't have to force anyone against his or her will, You are free to do as You like.

Do I arrange things for people?

When You deem it good or when You choose to do it.

Do you think I do it for you?

Oh, yes. I'm sure of that. I've seen things arranged for me that are far beyond the realms of what most people would call mere chance. I know that You love me and are actively taking a part in my life and perfection. You would do this for any of us who were sincere and dedicated to loving You and following You.

And what if you chose to go on a picnic and it rains?

Then I will understand that the earth is dry, and I shall love the rain for it nourishes the earth.

And when you catch the flu?

I get the rare opportunity to suffer some slight inconvenience and offer it to You in reparation for my sins and the sins of all mankind. Suffering is a great gift that You allow us if we know how to use it to advantage.

And what do you believe I have been demonstrating here as the third principle?

Everything beyond my own choices is chosen or influenced for me by God Himself. If I love God and am in His favor, everything beyond my own choice is chosen to be the best possible thing for all concerns, and especially me. That sounds kinda familiar; didn't St. Francis say that?

Yes. I give the truth to all who are dedicated to the truth and wish to hear it. Knock and it shall be opened, seek and ye shall find.

I get it. I know of many books that You have guided me to that contained great wisdom and truth.

Yes. I willingly use any avenues available to Me to assist My loved children to be what they can be. I have inspired many writers since the earliest times. All through the centuries I have inspired people to learn the truth and teach it to others. It is My way.

I remember; You usually teach through chosen people. You choose those who love You deeply and faithfully, then You teach through them. Why don't You just teach most people individually, like You did me?

Two reasons: they won't listen, and I choose to teach through chosen persons so that those teachers will get the merit of having done My will. It pleases a father to have one of his children teach some of his less advanced children, under his careful supervision.

I get that. That's a marvelous way to teach!

Naturally—I'm a marvelous guy, remember? (Chuckles.)

(Laughs.) Yeah, I remember.

So, review the first three principles we have covered.

Okay.

One—You **LOVE** me.

Two—Good things happen to me when I love You.

Three—You arrange things for me in my best interests.

And what other valuable things have you learned?

One—God **IS** Love.

Two—Love only takes care of needs and gives pleasure.

Three—Love is unreasonable.

Four—THE TRUTH IS: God is man's servant by His choice.

And how do you think others who will read this will take it?

Some will appreciate the good that is within it and learn from it. Some will not understand it because they choose to not understand it. Some will dislike it and attempt to find as many faults in it as they can. Some will attack it and me for writing it. Most will just ignore it.

And how will you feel when others attack you because of it?

Pleased. I don't expect most others will openly accept that I speak to You on a casual basis, and whenever I want to.

Why?

Because I'd probably think a person was crazy if they made that claim to me.

Why?

For the same reason as all of our other central problems—false beliefs.

Like what?

We've been taught that you just don't talk casually to God whenever you want to. If you claim to, you're crazy as a bedbug!

Do you care what others think of you or say to you?

Some, but not much. My only real concern is how **You** feel about me. I don't have to give any sort of accounting to other people—I have to with You.

And what accounting will you give to Me when the time comes?

That I have loved You all that I could, and desired to love You more. That I have loved my fellow man as You have taught me to. And that I have followed Your instructions as best I could, like writing out these conversations. That I have fulfilled my personal mission in life; I have taught all those who You sent to learn from me who remained sincere.

And what will you do when others dis-accept, disapprove, and attack you because of Me?

I will be filled with joy, for You have already told me of it. I count it as a blessing to be worthy of attack for my faith.

What else?

I shall be sad.

Why?

Because I know how much You love me.

So?

You will go very hard on those who attack me without just cause. I shall feel sorry for them if they are acting out of fear, jealousy, or some other false reasoning.

What if they are right?

You mean, what if I <u>am</u> crazy or I am just imagining that I am talking to You?

Yes.

Then it won't really matter. If what I write is true and good, it doesn't matter where it came from. What is good is good. You shall still go hard on those who attacked me if this work is good or true. If I read a book with great wisdom in it but I refuse to accept any of the good in it that could really help me just because I happen to disagree with the author's personality or views, then it is I who am at a loss and foolish.

By what authority do you teach?

By Your authority, or by my own imagination that I am convinced is You.

So if others refuse you and your teachings?

That is not my concern; loving and following You is.

I love you.

And I love You.

I assure you, many will read this and realize that what you put down here is true, and is of Me. Many are like you, Peniel, pilgrims here on earth, searching for truth and meaning. I shall touch some of them through this, and other works, and they shall recognize My hand. I will give many the courage to contact you to learn more of the truth, and many of those who are looking for Me will come to you so that you can point the way for them to start returning to themselves. And some will find your work their mission also, and they will assist you to guide others to the truth and love.

That would be great. I can't wait! It will be so nice to have some serious and sincere people to learn with. You have already taught me so many important truths that just can't be adequately put on paper. And I have other important things to do, like loving You and perfecting myself.

I know. Don't worry; your time is coming. For now, write down the things that I tell you to and I will arrange the rest.

Okay, I'm writing.

Perhaps we shall publish this along with some other selected writings and things you have gotten from other books and people. It could help a lot of people and it would please Me.

Yeah, but what about those who will read it and think I'm kooky? They'll bother Gail and Summer.

Don't worry. I love you, and if other people think you're kooky, then that will keep you from getting a swelled head. Some will be jealous of you, and some will be afraid of you because you threaten their dearly held false beliefs. It was the same way for Me when I was on earth.

I just want for others to be able to love You as best they can. I have been shown so much that could help others, I wish for them to learn of it.

I know how eager you are. Have patience for now. All things come to he who waits patiently.

Okay, I'll slow down when I teach others. I know that I get excited most of the time when someone is really learning something important—I start talking fast and going overboard, pushing too hard.

You can do Me a great service. There are thousands of serious seekers just waiting for someone to show them the way. You will help many of them.

I can't wait!

I love you, sweet Peniel.

And I love You more than my own life and happiness.

CHAPTER 5

What Man Wants

Me: I love You.

God: And I love you.

It seems like it means a lot more now. I won't use the term lightly in the future.

Good. Many people use the term love without ever knowing just how important it really is.

I understand.

Let's talk more about God's relationship with man.

Okay.

What do you want to do for Summer?

Mostly, I want to love her—take care of her needs and give her as much pleasure as she is willing to accept.

Would you ever force her to receive these gifts against her will?

No. I give her complete freedom first, then these gifts.

Why do you love her?

There is no reason to love; otherwise love would be impure.

Good—it pleases Me to know that you understand this.

Yeah, I love her because I choose to; I choose to love her because it is good to love her and I choose to do what is good.

And what do you get from loving another person?

Fulfillment. And I get to be Goooood (God) for them and to them. It gives me pleasure and satisfaction. But these are not why I love, they are just added bonuses. I would still love even if I didn't get anything from it.

Very good. You have a clear understanding of this, I see. You realize what it is like to love, that is, you realize what it is like to be Goooood (God).

If there were a choice about which to do first—take care of needs or give pleasure—which would you do first?

I would take care of needs first. It does little good to tell someone a joke to cheer them up when they have no food. You would give them the food first.

Correct. So would you say that taking care of needs is priority over giving pleasure and takes precedence?

Yes.

How long would you wait until you would be willing to take care of one of Summer's true needs?

I wouldn't wait. I'd do it as soon as the need developed. To withhold something that I can easily give is cruel and wrong.

And what about Me? Would I hesitate to give you what you truly needed if you asked it of Me and you were in My favor?

Certainly not.

Would there ever be a reason why you might not give Summer something that she asked you for?

Oh yes. Many times she asks for something that she really doesn't need or that isn't good for her to have. I would always give her what she truly needs if she asks for it, but I don't give her everything she asks for.

Give Me an example that we can work with.

Okay. I wouldn't give her four pounds of candy if she asked for it.

Nor would I. However, let's say that she keeps begging and asking and whining as kids sometimes do. What would you do then?

It depends on my mind at the time. I might just give it to her to teach a lesson—if she weren't willing to listen to reason.

What lesson?

Not everything you ask for is in your best interests. Sometimes people convince themselves that they desire something, but after they get it, they find it is not good for them.

What if Summer had asked you for a gun and some bullets instead of four pounds of candy?

I would never give a five-year-old a gun.

Why not?

It would be very dangerous for her. She doesn't have the wisdom to use it properly yet.

Even if she asks for it incessantly?

Never. I would not give any person anything that I thought could be deadly to them.

And neither would I. Do you understand why some prayers get answered and some don't?

Yes, I see it clearly. Knowing that You act just like any good loving father is very helpful in understanding Your actions and motives.

Won't Summer be upset if she doesn't get what she asks you for, knowing full well that you could give it to her easily?

Perhaps. I see Your point. I guess the biggest problem concerning prayers of request is that most of us just don't know what is good for us.

Yes. This does cause many problems.

If Summer really knew that four pounds of candy was bad for her, she probably would stop asking for it. Really understanding what is good for us and what is not would be very helpful. How do we discover what is really good for us?

By understanding what you really want, not what you desire or think you want. Many times you think that you really want something and you mistakenly believe that it is good for you when it is merely a base desire of your flesh and is harmful to you.

I see. I know that it is very rare that we choose to <u>want</u> what we believe is bad or harmful to us. So the problem lies in better understanding of what is not good for us. Yeah, just like everything else, this is tied up with all those false beliefs. If we didn't have any false beliefs, then we wouldn't falsely believe that something was really good for us when in fact it wasn't!

Very good. Give Me an example.

Like, I might believe that I want sex five times a day and that it would be good for me. But this would probably just be the need for attention disguised in the clothing of sexual urges. What I might really want is to get a little more attention, a little more love.

Very good. So how do you come to the point where you will only ask for what you really want, and not what you just desire?

When you really love yourself and overcome your false beliefs.

Super. How do you do this?

Well, I can simply ask You and You will guide me.

Yes, however many of the people reading this are not yet able to hear Me like you are. How can they best do this?

They can reason for themselves. Find out what is ultimately best for them in the overall sense, and then want to acquire just these things.

Like what?

Oh, that's simple. Everyone really wants the same things. We have covered this before: **Nirvana**—success—well-being, and good fortune.

Let us go over the information as we did before for the advantage of those who will later read this.

Okay.

Which of these three should a person work on acquiring first?

Success. And when success is achieved it brings fulfillment.

Then what?

Since you are successful and fulfilled, well-being naturally follows—unless you prevent it.

And then?

Well-being gives you a very positive outlook and attitude. Usually the successful person will look for the higher things in life, such as a good relationship with You. Once a person establishes a good loving relationship with You, You send them good fortune.

All things work for the good of they who love the Lord.

Right. If loving You purely brings good fortune, and good fortune is the last step in getting what we really need, then the two previous steps must be tied up with learning to love You better.

Very good. And how do I desire for you to love Me?

Well, first You want me to allow You to love me in any way You choose, and not reject Your love.

And?

And then You want me to return Your love in as pure a way as I can.

And how is this done?

Through loving my neighbor.

And when you do love your neighbor, what actions do you perform for your neighbor?

The actions of love: taking care of his true needs and giving him all the pleasure that he is willing to receive.

And how is this loving accomplished?

You Yourself love that person through us, for You are the life and goodness within us that loves others. And it is through loving that person that I show him **Love**; that is, I show him **God**—the God that is within me—that I become for him when I love him.

And what does it do for he who is loved?

Well, for one thing it allows him to receive the love of God given through my loving of him. It **reveals** God to him through the actions of love, for the actions of love are always the actions of God. And it gives him the rare opportunity to love Jesus Christ through loving me, for I have become his neighbor through loving him, and You will have his actions toward me be directed toward You Yourself—for You have allowed me to become God for him through loving him and revealing the Goooood (God) that is within me to him.

And what does it do for he who is doing the loving?

It allows him to receive the merits and benefits of having loved. It allows him to have his love directed to one who needs it. It allows him the opportunity to love Jesus Christ by loving the goodness and life within the other person—for that goodness and life within him **IS You**. It gives him the ability to love better and easier next time he chooses to do so. It increases his capacity for love. It fulfills him. It gives his life meaning and direction. It fills him with joy. It even does all manner of good for him that he is unaware of. It reserves special merits and gifts for him in eternity. It pays back for some of the evil and sin he has committed against You, his neighbor, and himself. It makes the world a better place for him to live in—and the list could go on forever.

And if you allowed Me to love you, and loved Me in return through loving your neighbor, then what?

I don't know, is there more?

What about loving yourself?

Oh yeah. Well, you should love yourself better for four reasons.

What are they?

One: Because you are good and you deserve to be loved. It would be wrong to refuse to love someone as good as yourself.

And two?

Two: You should love yourself so that you will be more willing to receive the love of God, which is your primary reason for existing—and what God wants most for you. Many times we are not willing to receive all the love that God chooses to give us because we do not think we are worthy of it. We think these things because we do not love ourselves, as we should. Hence, this creates a barrier between the love of God and us as individuals.

Beautiful. And third?

Three: So that you will be more willing to receive the love of others. Just as it is with receiving the love of God, so it is with receiving the love of others. You will not receive it willingly and gracefully unless you feel worthy and deserving of it.

And fourth?

Four: So that you will be more able to give love to God and others. You will never be fully able or willing to love another until you completely love yourself. There's an old saying that torture is a sign of weakness and self-hate, for it is easy to hate and hurt—but it takes great courage to love and sacrifice. If you do not love yourself you will not be willing to give this precious gift to others. "Why should I give them love when nobody loves me?" the unloved person says to himself. And since he doesn't love himself, he is unwilling to receive love from others. He feels unloved and unwilling to love others. It is a vicious circle to get caught in.

So, what is the first step to take on the path back to perfection if one wishes to be perfect; or if he just wants to be better than he now is?

You should **learn to love yourself** better.

And then?

Accept what you have learned.

Then?

Apply what you have learned.

And then?

Don't make yourself fail and **don't ever quit**.

Why?

Because if you don't give up, make yourself fail, or hinder yourself, you will eventually accomplish your goal of loving yourself purely.

And what will be the results of that?

You will be a **success** in life! I get it. A success is a person who really loves himself.

Very good. A success is a person who gets what he really wants; and what everyone really wants is **to be loved completely**. You can never be loved completely until you love yourself completely, hence, when you do achieve loving yourself completely, you become a true success in life!

Is that all there is to being a true success in life?

No. Loving yourself completely makes you a success; yet, you can be a success and become very vain. A **total success** is he who loves himself perfectly so that he may love God through loving his neighbor.

I get it. Loving yourself is not the goal; it is just a necessary means to doing what is more noble—loving **You**.

Right. Anyone who loves himself purely is a success, and a total success goes beyond this to loving others perfectly.

And that explains what I have thought about a successful person. I believed that a success was a person that liked things just as they were and wouldn't want to change anything about his life or self. Basically, a success would be someone who really liked himself and his life. He really loves it, not just likes it.

Yes. The test of a true success is to ask him what he would change about himself or his life. If he would change anything, that means that he is not totally satisfied with things as they are; hence, he would rather they be different; hence, he does not fully love it.

So when a person is really a success, he no longer wants anything?

Right, remember the earlier discussions. We are merely building on them. You said that a success was a person who possesses all that he should in the proper amount. This is true; and the most important things to possess are things that come only when you love yourself purely.

Such as?

Peace, integrity, fulfillment, rapture, sincerity, and excitement in life. All the things that together make life great and are summed up by the term well-being.

I just figured something else out.

What's that?

Integrity—that means being more concerned about giving another person what they really need or want than making a buck off of them.

Such as?

Like a used car salesman that really wants to get you a good car that you will be happy with rather than trying to stick you with some junker and making a fast buck off you.

And?

Well, let's say that there is this salesman that is a real success. I say to him, "Man, that 2000 Prowler looks real nice and that $20,000 price seems very reasonable to me. Can we arrange for me to buy it"? But being a success he will say, "Peniel, that car was wrecked, and if you bought it, it would probably be just one long headache for you. I'll admit that the price seems fair, but there are several things wrong with the engine and I don't think that it would be a good car for you. Let's look at this 2001 Intrepid over here. Now I know that this is a good car and it is a real good buy…"

Yes. How would you feel if you met a used car salesman like that?

I'd be flabbergasted.

And what would you do?

I'd always come back to him whenever wanted another used car. I wouldn't deal with anyone else. I'd know that I could trust this guy and that he wasn't out to make a fast buck off me. I'd know he really cared about me and my needs and wants.

What else?

I'd tell all my friends about it; and, you can bet that if they ever want a used car they would remember it and probably come to him also.

And how will this work out for the salesman?

His dealer had better get a bigger lot, 'cause when the word gets around, he's going to get a lot of business. The salesman will be financially successful because of his integrity. He will have lifetime repeat customers who are faithful to him. And not only would they be his customers—they'd be his friends!

And remember another of the definitions of success you have been given?

Yes: A success is a person who establishes life-long relationships based on the principles of love and integrity.

And again, this ties in with loving your fellow man. If you love yourself purely then you can love others and establish these lifelong relationships. It is a shame isn't it?

What?

That there are so few true professionals in business today. To those who learn the secrets of success, professionalism naturally follows in their work. Professionalism is tied to being able to love your customer, also.

Yes, that is a shame.

A professional is a successful businessperson with personal integrity. There are many people who have achieved financial security and independence, yet are not successful at all.

Why not?

Because they feel guilty about how they have made their money. They made it by cheating, deceiving, or using other people. And if your fortune comes this way, I shall never let you fully enjoy it or be a real success. You shall still not like yourself. You may be rich, yet you will still be empty and unhappy.

So in the long run, a success is a person who loves himself.

Right. And all self-made successes got that way through loving others. A success is a person who has a lot of true friends.

And a complete success is a person who loves himself purely so that he can love others.

Right. And notice you don't have to love others in order to be a complete success; you just have to be able and willing. You can be a complete success in life and be a hermit who lives on a mountaintop with no one else around.

I get it—we are still dealing with motives, primarily.

Yes. If you had to actually love others actively in order to be a success, then you would have to have others around you who are willing to receive your intense love.

I see. If I really want and choose to love my fellow man perfectly and intensely, yet there are none around me at the time willing to receive my pure and intense love, I still gain the merit of it. Otherwise, I could be hindered from being all I choose because there was no one willing to receive my intense love. The merit resides in my motives and me only—no one can stop me but me!

Beautiful! Okay, sum up what you can.

1. The key to our purpose and reason for existence lies herein.

2. The ultimate goal is to be with God eternally.

3. The judgment for eternal salvation is based on loving God.

4. We cannot, as we now are, love God.

5. God has provided us with a way to love Him.

6. The way is to love our neighbor as ourselves.

7. God made us primarily so that He could love us.

8. Hence, God is the willing servant of man.

9. We have many false beliefs that are the core of our problems.

10. Our neighbor is he who loves us.

11. Love is **God.**

12. Love takes care of needs and gives pleasure only.

13. Substitute feels and acts as God does toward for love.

14. Love is defined as the personality of God.

15. All people want the same thing—Nirvana.

16. Nirvana is success, well-being, and good fortune.

18. Success is loving yourself purely.

19. Success brings fulfillment.

20. A total success is he who loves himself in order to love others.

21. A successful person establishes life-long relationships based on love.

22. Fulfillment brings with it well-being.

23. Well-being is a good relationship with God.

24. Well-being brings good fortune.

25. Good fortune means having God's favor.

That is very good. I'm very proud of you. You have come far.

Thank You for teaching me. I hope many people will gain some good and deeper understanding from all of this.

It has been well worth recounting these old conversations if they just help you alone. Right?

Right. I love You, Dad!

And I love you also, Peniel.

CHAPTER 6
Twelve Reasons Why Man Exists

Me: Dad, why we are here?

God: I shall give twelve reasons why people exist in the order in which they usually occur chronologically in life. Here are the twelve reasons why man exists:

1. To be loved by God.
2. To be loved by others.
3. To be aware of others.
4. To be aware of self.
5. To love self.
6. To love others.
7. To be aware of God.
8. To love God.
9. To fulfill your personal mission in life.
10. To be God for others.
11. To perfect your love and love all good.
12. To die.

Let us speak about each of these.

Okay. These are the central reasons why any person is created. The first one is always the principle reason why I create any person, as we have already discussed.

Teach me the core of what it means to be loved by God.

It means that I made you to take care of you and give you as much pleasure as possible.

If this is true, why is there such suffering and inhumanity in the world?

The reason is because I gave all of you your freedom to choose. I will not force these wonderful destined gifts on anyone. The world is in a pitiful state because man's spirit is in a pitiful state.

You mean man's personality is in a pitiful state.

Yes, exactly. If most people really chose to be sincere, loving, benevolent people, do you think that your world would be changed for the better?

I don't know. It seems that there are a few people who make most of the decisions for the majority of the people. If those people who exert a lot of major influence were to become benevolent and sincere and have true personal integrity, then that might make a great difference.

We shall cover this in a later discussion on power. Let us keep to the subject for now.

Okay. If all men would choose to be good and loving, then the world would be a much better place.

And how about an individual's happiness in life?

It comes from willingly receiving Your love. If we were totally willing to receive Your service and gifts of pleasure, surely our lives would be joyous!

Yes, this is true. I will that each of My children have pleasure as I have destined for them in this mortal life. Yet, you know that pain and suffering are superior.

Yes, I remember our discussions on this.

We shall also recover them for the sake of the readers of this book—at a later time.

Okay, back to Your loving us.

My love for you begins at the moment I create you. The very act of creation itself is an act of My love. You are brought into existence by love (God), for love (God), to love. And what do you think man's true essence is made out of? If you could put a person's essence on the table and identify it, what would it be made of?

Love!

Exactly! I Myself AM Love, and when I created you, I made you out of Myself (Love); I made you out of the same essence that I Myself am. I was not made out of it, for I was not made; yet it is the essence of what God IS.

Man, I keep getting amazed at how far-reaching and meaningful the statement God IS Love is for me.

Good. Do you understand the basic premise of the first reason why a person exists—to be loved by God?

Yes. Let's talk about the second one—to be loved by others.

Okay.

When does this usually start in life—when we get attached to mother's womb and her body starts taking care of our needs?

No. That happens without her willing it. It is not yet an act of love. Love is involved with will and motive—remember?

Yes. So when does other's love for us start? When we are born?

Well, it could start while you are still in the womb, after your mother knows that you are there.

How can that be? She can't take care of your needs in the womb or give you pleasure.

Perhaps not, yet she can still do things out of love for you. Such as eating right because she loves you, or not smoking because she loves you. And even if she doesn't DO anything, it is the willingness to love that is really the important thing. Remember?

Yeah. If she really wants to take care of your needs and give you pleasure, then she loves you. Love doesn't have to do anything. Love is in the willingness and wanting to love.

Again, you see well. Love is intention, usually followed by action.

But does it have to be my mom?

No. Your mother is just usually the first one to be aware of you.

So my second reason for existing starts whenever any other person becomes aware of me?

Right. Then they can love you if they choose to.

I affect them?

Yes. You force them to make a decision to love you or to not love you. Until they are aware of you, you do not affect them in this way.

And some of Your children never reach this stage, do they?

That's right. Some of them are created by Me and then come to Me before any other person is aware that they ever existed. If this is My will for some, then it is good.

I see.

And when others do become aware of you, it allows them the opportunity to fulfill another of their reasons to exist—to love others.

I see—they all work together.

At least they can and should. They don't always work together because each of you is free to choose to do as you will.

And what about the third one—to be aware of others?

This means awareness itself. For a while, a baby does not have the mental capacity for awareness. When they do become aware of other's existence, they fulfill the next stage of reason for man's existence.

Why is awareness so important?

The main differences between man and beast are tied up with awareness. Awareness is what gives you the ability and power to choose. Without awareness of others, you could never respond to others; you could never love others.

Is this what we mean by conscious?

Basically; awareness is conscious awareness.

Is there such a thing as unconscious awareness?

Yes. For instance, the awareness of God starts out as an unconscious awareness. All children know that they had a creator, only most of them do not become conscious of this fact for a time.

Okay, I get that.

And now let's speak of the fourth reason for man's existence—to be aware of self.

Sure. This is a major step in the development of a human being—or we might say, a human BECOMING.

When does this come about?

When the child looks at his own hand and moves it and thinks, *Wow, I did that! I moved my hand. It's my hand and I control it!*

He gains power over his bag of tools.

Yes. That's a good analogy for the human body.

And there is a later problem with this aspect of being human, isn't there?

Yes. Sometimes when children grow up they lose touch with this vital fascination with their own power and being. They stop enjoying just being alive. It is sad. Life is too wonderful a gift to be taken so lightly by so many!

Yes. I remember how much good I got out of the Gestalt Therapy I did for myself. It is wonderful to rediscover the marvelous things about being truly aware of self and environment.

Yes. We shall assist some people in the future to regain a true awareness of the joy of being alive and powerful.

Super. That would please me a great deal.

Now let's talk about the fifth reason why man exists—to love self. I guess this is a pretty important step.

Yes. When a person first exerts his own power and free will to take care of his own needs rather than have a parent do it for him—and then feels the satisfaction that comes from loving self—this is a wonderful moment!

What does it mark in the development of the person?

It marks the beginning of true person-hood as an individual.

Let's talk about the sixth one—to love others.

Isn't it marvelous when a child chooses to buy their parent a birthday gift instead of spending their allowance on themselves?

Yes.

Oh, and the true fulfillment that they experience—perhaps for the first time. They have unselfishly loved another and it feels very good. It marks the beginning of fulfillment in life, if they choose to continue loving others unselfishly.

It is a shame that more parents do not accept their responsibility to teach their young children the really important things in life—such as these things. Someone ought to set them straight!

Have mercy and think no bad thoughts, My son. Most of them are not aware of what they are doing. They are aware that something is missing, yet they don't know where to look to find it. Remember to be forgiving of the ignorant, if their ignorance is unintentional.

Yes, I will remember.

And what about the seventh one—to be aware of God?

And here starts the really serious problems for most of My beloved children. For many, because of their environment and the beliefs taught to them while growing up, they have very serious misconceptions about Me.

Yes. I remember that my earthly father was a good, loving, religious man with a love for life and You; yet even with all of his goodness, he taught me many things about You that You have since cleared up for me. They were not grave errors and he did the best that he knew how to do. I only wish that he could have known the real You better.

Yes. And this is exactly the problem most people face. It is impossible to love that which you do not know, and the more misperceptions you have about a person, the less pure your attempts at loving them will be.

Yeah, I understand this. Before I really knew You, I found it very difficult to love You with a strong, pure love.

It's more than just believing that I do exist and that I am a good Creator, it's supposed to be a unique personal experience that leaves an unmistakable impression. Like the first time you met Santa.

Yes. I wish more people knew You better and could experience what **You ARE Love** really means. It would greatly improve their relationship with You if they just knew the real You better.

And now let's speak of the eighth reason for man's existence—<u>to love God</u>.

This is the biggy, isn't it?

Yes. After receiving My love for you, this is the second most important reason why I have created you. It makes Me very pleased when you return My love to Me. It makes you divine in nature.

But You know all the difficulties we have with loving You. We cannot love You directly. We cannot love You purely until we know You intimately. We find it difficult to love You because You seem so far removed from our everyday lives. We have a hard time loving ourselves purely and therefore are oftentimes unwilling to love You much at all. And the list of problems with our relationship with You could go on for pages and pages.

Yes, and man himself is fully responsible for all of these. Don't focus on the negative side of it. Look at it as a challenge that has been given for man to overcome and gain the merit of having won out in the battle for true purpose and fulfillment in life.

And how is this to be done?

You yourself have been taught much about how to guide other people seeking these exact things, have you not?

Yes, many of them. But it would be difficult to convey in words all of the important truths that You have shown me. They are simple, yes, and easy to learn, yet they cannot be adequately conveyed with a book.

And that is not our intention. I only intend for the readers of this to become aware that there is an answer and they can find it if they choose to and are sincere. Many of them will ignore all of this, yet it will touch some whom I have intended it for, and they shall seek and find these most important answers in life.

Where will they look?

Some of them will find the answers for themselves. I will further guide some of them alone. Many of them will seek you out to learn these things from you. I have not given your wisdom and teaching abilities for nothing. I shall use you a great deal if you will let me.

That would be great! I do will it.

Now we'll talk about the ninth reason why man exists—to fulfill personal mission in life.

This is where one of my favorite sayings comes in.

Which is...?

God doesn't make junk!

This is true. I put a great deal into the creation of each individual; each of you is worth more than the entire non-human universe. I have chosen almost everyone who will eventually be reading this book to have a most important and noble destiny. I have great things in mind for each of you to accomplish in life. I didn't make you to sit around watching television all of the time. There are so many important things that I wish for you to do for Me.

Why do you not know this? Why have you treated so lightly the gifts I have given you? When will you accept that I am your Father and I have a mission for you? I shall not let any other person do the work that I have destined for you to do. Since you are still unwilling, your important work goes undone. You would receive such joy and fulfillment if you would only accept your own destiny and purpose.

I shall never let you be truly satisfied until you come to be what you can be! Don't you know why you sometimes think, *is this all there is? Isn't there something more to life than this?* Together we have such wonderful work to do. There are so many important things to be done that only you, dear reader, can do. Please allow yourself the golden opportunity to be what you truly want to be: loved and fulfilled.

I didn't destine you to be as you now are; I destined you for greatness—it awaits only your sincere decision to find your purpose in life. I will take it from there and guide you. Please accept your personal destiny.

The consequences of your refusing Me again will be very grave for you in the future—don't refuse Me. Let Me love you and guide you. Life will be marvelous and fulfilled when you finally accept your personal destiny.

That's very moving. I hope that it will touch many.

Now let us speak of the tenth reason why I have created you—<u>to be God for others</u>.

Yeah, what do You mean by that. Aren't You God for us?

I was once told, "Your mother and brothers are waiting outside to see you." And I replied to this statement, "Who is My mother and brother? He who does the will of My Father in heaven—he is My family!"

So what is Your point?

You are allowed to be God for another person when you choose to allow the Goooood (God) within you to come forth in your motives and actions. You may be God for another person by sincerely loving them—for loving is all that God does. Anyone who loves is <u>of God</u>.

Like when we have children or give a stranger a lift or anything like that.

Yes. For this is the will of My Father, that you love Us and love your neighbor as yourself.

That's beautiful. I shall remember this, always.

And what about the eleventh reason why we exist—<u>to perfect Your love and love all that is good</u>?

Perfect love casts out all fear. I desire for all of My children to be fearless. And remember, I am all good. Whatever is good is I Myself. I exist within it and am present within it, if it is good. I should be recognized within all good and loved within all good.

But how can I love a rock? I know that the rock is good and You are in it, but I cannot give it service and pleasure.

No. Yet you do not have to perform any actions to love. You can appreciate the rock for its beauty and perfection and My presence, and in this way FEEL love for the rock. You can only really show the actions of love towards another person. All of the rest of nature may be appreciated and revered and used wisely and left in My wise keeping. In this way, man may show his love for nature.

Love may be felt towards anything at all. All good should be loved through appreciation and proper use. If you do not love something that is good, you have not yet achieved perfection. At perfection, all things are seen in Me and I am seen in all things. Remember how it was when you attained it?

Yes, I remember. I developed a love for all things. It is truly a wonderful state to be in—the state of naturalness. Yet, there are still times that I slip back into my old self; I wish it were not so.

Do not be concerned. Follow Me. You will overcome even these relapses.

That will be great. I wish people understood perfection as I now do.

We will cover this in a later talk also.

And now I shall cover the last reason why man exists—<u>to die</u>.

I already know Your views on this. They are beautiful!

Yes. If people understood death, they wouldn't fear or dislike it.

But it would be tough to write all that You have taught me about it.

OK, we will just touch upon it.

How do most people feel about death?

They hate, fear, and misunderstand it.

Yes. I will just say a little about it here. If the reader is serious about better understanding it, he may come and speak with you about it. As man is now, without death, he could not come to be with Me. If a person has lived a good life and accepted his personal destiny and done what I intended him to do, then death will be a welcome friend to him. It will be as the river raft captain that will bring him across the final river, to come to his eternal reward and resting place. If he is sure of his good standing with Me, he has no reason to fear death. Death is a part of life as it is now, though I did not intend it this way. Man himself chose death rather than Me. Only those who fear their own choices in life fear death. Nothing is more tragic than to come to death's door, only then to realize that you have never really lived at all!

I remember that You usually refer to what we call death as sleep.

Yes. Death is not as terrible as people think; it is very like sleep.

And you wake from sleep.

As you will wake from death!

Well, it's been a good talk. I so enjoy the pleasure of Your company.

Thank you very much. I enjoy speaking with you and will be very glad when I finally speak to others through you.

I love You, my wonderful Jesus. Praise be Your holy name!

I love you also, Peniel. Continue following Me. You are doing well.

CHAPTER 7

Man's Single Largest Problem

God: I love you, Peniel.

Me: And I love You too, Dad.

Let's talk about helping man.

Okay. What about helping man?

How can I do the most good for those whom You send to me to be taught about the truth?

By assisting them to overcome man's single largest problem and barrier to My love. If this major barrier can be overcome, then their life can be much better, richer, happier, and more productive.

Super—what is man's single biggest problem?

He doesn't love himself, as he believes he is. To be frank, most of you don't even like yourselves very much.

I have often noticed this. Why is it this way?

Two main reasons: guilt and false beliefs.

Shall we talk about guilt first?

Yes. Guilt is probably the smaller of the two, yet it has the larger impact because it is emotional in nature. False beliefs are responsible for many of your self-debasing actions, yet guilt is the result that comes from accepting and operating from these false beliefs.

Why do we have such feelings of guilt?

Because most of the time you think that you are not doing what you should be doing. You believe that your everyday life is a waste.

Yes, I remember well that feeling. Until You straightened me out, that underlying guilt feeling always pursued me-undermining my works, hurting my feelings, souring my personality. I know that this guilt is responsible for the way most people lead their everyday lives: in QUIET DESPERATION! But if we feel that our life is a wreck and that we are responsible and guilty, to whom do we say, "I'm sorry. Help me out of this mess I've made of my life."

Indeed, whom do you ask forgiveness from? Very few are willing to consciously ask Me, and they won't ask themselves.

Why are they unwilling to ask You?

Fear.

Fear about what?

Fear that I might reject them, fear that I'm not real, fear that they have no purpose in life, fear of what others might think about them if they spoke with Me, fear of the unknown, fear that their situation is hopeless, fear that I am not listening, fear others will laugh, fear of having to change—fear of everything.

Why won't they ask forgiveness of themselves?

Because they fully believe that they won't receive forgiveness from themselves.

Why wouldn't they forgive themselves?

Because they believe that they just don't care about themselves. They think that if they did care, they wouldn't have let themselves be dragged where they now are. They would treat themselves better and not do the destructive things that they keep doing to themselves and others.

And the other reason they won't forgive themselves is they believe that they don't deserve forgiveness. They say, "I'm just going to go out and do this same thing again and again; there's no use forgiving Myself, I know that I won't change—I'll keep doing this same old thing."

That's terrible. I remember having just those thoughts many times after I would commit one of my common sins. I wouldn't even ask my own forgiveness because I knew that I was going to do this sin again in the future.

Yes, it is very common.

And what about the second problem: false beliefs?

Well, much of the guilt stems from false beliefs. If you have accepted the false belief that some natural activity is sinful, bad, dirty, wrong, or the equivalent, then, when you do this perfectly natural action, you will feel guilty—and wrongly so. If you feel guilty over things that are not really wrong or bad, what good does it do you?

None—feeling guilty never does any good.

No, it doesn't. Yet parents were taught by their parents to instill the feelings of guilt in a child and then use this as a weapon. They use it against their children's natural urges, instincts, and actions. And these children learn from their parents how to instill feelings of guilt in others to modify their actions. It is a terrible circle.

Yes, I see. I still do this with Summer. I make her feel guilty over something based solely on my beliefs about what is moral and right and good. If I'm mistaken, I may be doing a lot of irreparable harm to her.

True. Yet most parents do it automatically, without thinking—out of mere habit.

And through her guilt forced on her by me, Summer adopts the same false beliefs that I am using to make her feel guilty over and over again.

Right. It is not exclusive to parents. Spouses do it to each other; children do it to their parents (after they learn how to); friends, acquaintances, lovers, religious leaders, and bosses do it—any relationship is susceptible to this disease.

But how can I come to realize which beliefs are good and right and which ones are false beliefs taught to me by others?

Love and reason are your guides. If it is unreasonable or contrary to the ways of love, it is a false belief.

Is that because all of Your wishes for us are loving or reasonable?

Exactly. False beliefs are beliefs that do not agree with My beliefs. My beliefs are always the true beliefs, for I am THE TRUTH.

If I propose a few beliefs will You assist me with the process of examining whether they are true or false beliefs so that I may get a little practice?

Sure. Give Me an example of a belief that you are uncertain about.

Okay. The belief that <u>a person should cry at a funeral if it was someone close to you who died</u>.

Yes. Many of these beliefs never get stated in so many words, yet they get taught through example and demonstration.

What about it? Is it a true or false belief?

Let's ask some leading questions to find out.

Okay.

Why would you cry?

You would cry because you feel sad or bad.

Why?

You would feel sad or bad because someone whom you loved is gone.

Where have they gone?

Well, if you believe that they were a good person and in God's favor, then you would believe that they have gone to heaven.

And is this a bad place?

No, it's a wonderful place to go.

So why are you so sad if this person has gone to a wonderful place?

Because you wish they were still here with you.

Even though you know that they are far happier where they are, you wish for them to be back here with you in a place that is not nearly as good? That sounds very selfish to Me.

I guess it is selfish to wish they were still here, if you believe that they are in heaven now. We cry because we want them here with us; because they gave us pleasure and we miss the pleasure we got from being with them. We are more concerned over our own satisfaction and desires than we are over the deceased person's happiness where they are. It's selfish! That's not in keeping with love. Love is never selfish. If we really loved the person, we would be glad that they had finally gone to their just reward. We should be rejoicing and having a party because someone that we loved has finally won life's race and attained the final prize—heaven.

Yes, this is usually the case. However, it is reasonable to experience their leaving as a true loss. The loss should be that here was a person that I loved dearly, and now I may no longer love them. This would be a reason for experiencing the loss unselfishly.

Yeah, but I don't know very many people who cry at a funeral because they miss giving the deceased person pleasure and service; they mostly cry because they experience the loss of pleasure themselves, or else they have just been taught that you should cry at funerals.

Alas, it is this way many times. It does not have to be this way for you any longer, for now you know the truth.

But if I smile at a funeral and am happy that good 'ol Joe is dead, they will think that I am cruel and insensitive.

So? You cannot control what others think. Which is better: to have others think well of you, or to be true to yourself and your own personal beliefs?

It is far superior to be true to yourself.

And if you pretended to be sad and cry when in fact you were happy, just because you didn't want others to think badly of you?

You would be a hypocrite. I see.

Now what do we talk about?

I've got an idea. Why don't You tell me what the two most common and damaging false beliefs are. If I fully understood these, I could do a great deal by assisting people to overcome these two.

You are remembering earlier conversations, right?

Yes, that's why I asked for two; I remember how these two were tied together and I thought it would be good to cover them here.

Good, we shall discuss them as we did before.

I know they are no secret. Many people already know these two widely held false beliefs and know how awesomely damaging they are, but many are still unaware of them. Which is the most damaging of these two worst false beliefs?

This belief: My situation determines how I feel, think, and act. This has never been even remotely true, yet most of you have always been taught this. You cannot see any aspect of society where this belief is not held. But everyone can reason it out for himself or herself, as we shall do here, and the truth becomes readily apparent.

You mean that no matter what situation I am in, I am still completely free to think, feel, and act any way I choose?

Yes. Everyone knows this is true. Most of the time, however, people act as if just the opposite were true. They act as if their environment were responsible and in control of their emotions, thoughts, and actions.

And we say very common things that reinforce this idea such as, He made me so mad, or I feel bad when this happens.

Yes. The normal conversations of everyday life are full of references to this most commonly held and damaging belief. It's very difficult to find any person who is free of this false belief.

What about certain situations that always "make" people angry?

Like what?

Like having a flat tire.

And most people would get very angry or frustrated because of this?

Yes; having a flat tire makes **me** mad!

No it doesn't.

Why do You say that?

If having a flat tire really did MAKE you mad, then every time you had a flat tire you would HAVE to get mad.

And I always do.

You always get mad because you always make yourself mad.

No; the flat tire makes me mad.

Is it possible that you could have a flat tire and be happy about it?

Yes. If I was in a really good mood and I didn't care about getting somewhere. Or if I wanted to have a flat tire—like I had bank robbers in the car with me that had abducted me, and there were police on the way.

I thought that having a flat tire made you mad?

Not if I choose to be happy.

Can you always choose to be happy even if you have a flat tire?

Yes, I guess I always have that choice.

No matter what situation you are in?

Yes. I am free to choose my emotions and thoughts any time I choose to. No one or no situation can force me to feel or act or think a certain way. I have total free will in these things.

And this is the truth of the situation. You can choose—always. It's just that most people are so used to running their lives as if their environment and other people controlled them, they forget that they really can take back their power of choice. They become unaware that there is any choice, so they don't choose. They have gotten used to the false belief that things outside of themselves really control their feelings and attitude and actions.

And we have given up our most vital and important power—the power to be master of ourselves.

Yes. A man becomes a sheep when he gives his free will away to other people or to the environment. He becomes a robot programmed by his beliefs. He thinks that other people and things control his every act, feeling, and thought. He says, "That makes me mad. This makes me happy. That is why I feel this way. I always feel this way about that. This is just the way I am. If you really loved me you'd..." and he is never willing to accept the responsibility for his own life.

Okay, I'm clear on this one. What is the second biggest false belief that is commonly held among people that causes a great deal of harm?

This belief: I can control the way another person feels, thinks, or acts.

This is almost the same as the first one. Are they related?

Yes; they work hand in hand. The first one makes more false beliefs for you; the second one makes you feel guilty.

I see how the first one creates new false beliefs, but how does the second one cause such guilt?

If you think that you have made your mother very unhappy, you feel guilty about it.

I get it. This is one of the main ways parents instill guilt.

Yes. They convince their children that they can control how the parent feels. If this is true, then the child is responsible for the way that the parent feels.

Give me a typical example to illustrate it.

Okay. A mother sees her child refusing to mind her. So, to use a more powerful weapon to alter the child's behavior, she resorts to guilt.

How?

She cries and tells the child that the child has MADE her unhappy BECAUSE the child won't mind.

And that makes the child believe that it is responsible for the way the parent feels in this case.

Yes. It is very effective—and very damaging to the child. The parent usually is unaware of the evil they are doing.

And it's not just parents and children, is it?

No. Like the first false belief, any relationship is susceptible to this disease also.

I see Your point here—but what about the other side of the coin? Can I make someone happy?

No.

How can You say that?

I can say it because it is the truth.

You mean I can't make Gail or Summer or anyone happy?

No. You cannot make another happy—not at all.

I thought I could.

Well, they could be happy if they want to, but you can't make them happy. If they really chose to be sad and gloomy, could you force them against their will to feel a certain way?

No, I guess not. Not if it is true that any person can be in full charge of his emotions if he chooses to be.

And that is true and you know that it is. You just don't want to admit the truth of the matter that you can't make another person happy. No one can. Even I can't FORCE anyone to be happy unless I were to remove their free will and choice; and if I did that they would no longer be human, because having free will is one of the defining aspects of what it means to be human.

It's very hard to accept that I can't make another person happy.

And neither can you make him mad, or jealous, or hateful, or spiteful—or any emotional state at all. They have total free will—IF THEY CHOOSE TO HAVE A CHOICE.

I think I see what You're driving at; they do let me make them happy because they have turned over their choice of how they feel to me!

Yes. You DO NOT MAKE them happy, they allow you to do it. The choice is always ultimately theirs. They just usually allow themselves to be happy as a result of your actions. YOU don't make them happy; they ALLOW themselves to be happy because of you.

I get it. And another person allows himself to get angry because of something I did.

Yes. And he acts as if he had no choice in his emotions and he says that you were solely responsible for his anger. He says, "You made me mad because of what you did!"

And he is mistaken. He got mad because he chose to. I was just the excuse he used to justify his anger.

This is very good. And everyone else believes that you are to blame for his anger, also. It's a conspiracy that is agreed with from almost every side.

And it is not true at all!

It is certainly not. If he really wanted to be happy and he chose to be happy, it would be impossible for you to stop him! And, if he chose to be mad, regardless of what you did, he will get mad and you cannot stop him. No one may force any other person to feel any emotion at all. Yet, this is the widely held belief!

Well then, what can I do? I will to make others happy, but I know that I cannot force them. What should I do?

First, know that you are not responsible for how others feel; THEY are. Second, be aware that few other people know this truth. Third, know that most people will usually turn over their power to you if you are willing to "make" them happy, but the choice is still really theirs. Fourth, do everything in your power to **create an atmosphere conducive to others being most able to choose for themselves to be happy!**

I see. Basically it works as if I did control their feelings and emotions because they have surrendered this power to me. BUT the power is still theirs and they can take it back at will. If they become happy and say that I have made them happy, I will understand the truth.

Which is?

That it is really they that have chosen for themselves to be happy; they just mistakenly believe that I have been the cause of their joy. I will be pleased that they are happy, but I will know the truth of the matter.

And what if they become angry and blame their anger on your actions?

I will know the truth in this instance also.

Which is?

They have chosen to be angry and are just using my actions as an excuse to justify their anger. If they really didn't want or choose to be angry, they don't have to. I am not responsible for how another person feels—THEY ARE!

And how will you respond?

I will respond as I always do—with love. For I realize that they are still unaware of their deception. And I will still create an environment conducive to their happiness, and it will still be their choice to be happy or mad. I will not allow myself to be bullied into guilt because of their commonly held false belief—I know the truth!

And when someone lays a guilt trip on you, what will you do?

Understand. And love them. And if they are receptive to the truth and wish to learn it, I shall teach them.

And if you teach them the truths like this one, what will they gain from the truth?

They shall know the truth and the truth shall set them free.

Free from what?

Free from themselves and suffering. Free from their undeserved guilt. They will finally be free from the false beliefs that are the source of most of their troubles, worries, guilt, shame, hatred, unhappiness, and feelings of being unfulfilled. Free from their old self.

And this is a wonderful thing, to be freed from all of the games and masks and lies and false beliefs and deception and trouble. You have a marvelous and important job ahead of you: to teach THE TRUTH to many of My children who will seek you out.

But we have been talking for years, and You have taught me so many important truths like this one. I cannot teach each person all of them. There are hundreds and hundreds!

I know. I don't expect you to teach everything that I have taught you to every person I send to you. I will tell you what is good to teach each when the time is right. Trust Me.

I do. But why have You taught me so much?

For the same reason that you are usually willing to teach any person so much—because you love them and you enjoy teaching. Even if there is no practical application for a thing you may teach them, it is enjoyable just to understand the truth deeper. I love you and enjoy teaching you. You always listen to Me with an open mind and you treat Me with respect and reverence. If any person does all this for you, you are obligated to teach him anything that he desires to learn! This is why I have taught you so much.

There will be many who will come to learn and they each have different needs. You will have to fulfill the need to teach each according to what his needs are. Most of them have very common needs when you first start teaching them, for most have the same false beliefs to overcome and operate from the same set of misconceptions. After they advance in their learning a great deal, then their needs will vary. This is the reason why you have been shown so much.

I see. Should I transcribe some of the other writings and books that You have instructed me to write?

In time you will publish some of the others. I will tell you which books and writings to publish and when. Trust Me.

I do, and You know that. I just want to keep everything straight in my mind. I know that You are guiding me and You know best. I am fulfilled when I am teaching a willing, sincere disciple these things, for I know that this is my destiny and purpose for the future; yet, I gain the greatest pleasure from speaking with You. You are all to me; I love You more than life itself!

I know. I love you also. Peace be to you, Peniel.

CHAPTER 8

Why Man Is Not His Natural Self

Me: Dad, what should I teach someone when he first comes to me to learn?

God: Nothing. First, put them at ease.

Shouldn't I teach them something to prove that I have the ability to teach the truth?

No. You have nothing to prove, and a real seeker should not be interested in proof—only in truth.

Is this why You oftentimes refused to perform miracles when people specifically requested some sign?

Sometimes—it is a vile age that asks for signs. I didn't perform miracles sometimes because people tried to make it a circus-like atmosphere—I dislike foolish shows of ego or wrongful pride.

I know. What then should I do to put the person at ease?

Tell them a joke, buy them a coke, give them a poke—show them that you are just like anyone else. Many may later approach you and want to put you on a pedestal or make out that there's something different or unique about you. Do not be changed by other people's attitude toward you; you know how easily many are fascinated.

Yeah, I've already had a little trouble like this; I noticed when I taught Raccaab and Yentzel that I got the idea that they thought differently of me once they found out about some of my mystical experiences and visions and stuff.

Yes. People still view these natural sides of humanity with curious fascination. A good example is the immediate thoughts that come to their minds when they hear the words prophet or mystic.

Yes. These words conjure up visions of devout holy monks fasting on a mountaintop and being very abnormal.

(Laughs.) Yes, that's pretty close to what they think. Perhaps they think that a person stops being a "person" when he becomes a prophet or a mystic. I guess that these flights of their imagination stem from their mistaken impressions of what these people are really like. It's much the same problem as there is with people knowing the real Me. They think I am unfathomable or beyond comprehension!

Yeah. They're all in for a big surprise when they finally meet You.

So, Peniel, the first thing to do is to put them at ease and do your level best to dispel any strong misperceptions about you they may have developed from reading your books or hearing about you. It's not a big problem for you, yet, because your time has not yet come; it may become a problem in the future.

Is it my problem?

No. It will be the problem of the person with the false beliefs, as usual. But it will be a problem for you in that it may deter from your ability to reach and teach this individual effectively. I had much the same problem when I came, remember?

Yeah. You wouldn't even tell them plainly who You really were. You let them discover it for themselves as they came to really know You personally.

And the reason was that they already had all these false beliefs about Me. They thought they knew just what the personality of God was like, and they thought they had really figured out what the Messiah was going to be like and what I'd do. Boy, were they mistaken!

So, how were things affected by this misunderstanding?

Well, if I'd just stepped out when My time had come and announced to everyone everywhere that I was the Son Of God, the Messiah come! they would have immediately put on Me their preconceived ideas of what I was like.

Just like we project upon God after we find out that our parents weren't our creators. The earlier decisions about God that we made get projected onto God when we finally do meet Him.

Exactly, and this is what would have happened. I went back to My hometown and announced who I was to those that had known Me in My earlier life, before it was My time, and they ran Me out of town and were going to throw Me off a cliff; My own townsfolk!

A prophet is never welcome among his own, huh?

A prophet is very rarely welcome anywhere. The people that think they really knew you, find it difficult to accept that you are really different, and many of them simply believe that you are faking or putting on airs.

Yes. I don't expect that my family members and people who think they really know Mark well to accept Peniel with ease and grace; I realize that it will be difficult for many of them.

You always have Me!

Thank God for that!

You're welcome. Now, back to the original discussion. What will you do when you first encounter one whom you suspect I may have brought to learn from you?

I shall put them at ease and go a little overboard to show them that I'm just a regular Joe, like anyone else. I hate when a person puts me up somewhere above himself or herself.

Why?

You know why: mainly because it is much more difficult to love them and teach them and reach them from up there! I would much rather them let me stay down with them so that I could speak casually with them. Formality is so stupid sometimes!

Yes. Rituals can lose their meaning and become a hindrance to love! Spontaneity is always good, and love is very spontaneous!

I know You are!

You remember that I am Love. Good!

Okay, so I have spent a little time and put them at ease and shown them that I'm human and just a regular guy—then what?

Well, you will do what you feel compelled to do. It will vary from one person to the next.

I know, but what would be a typical example?

Well, you might establish your credentials by allowing them to ask you some question that they really want to know the answer to, and then give them your views and an explanation of what they mean.

Yes, that might be very good to do. What else might I do?

You could speak casually with them for a little while to discover their intentions and what they would have you do for them.

Yes, that could be beneficial.

And you could simply ask them a bunch of leading questions to draw out of them the things that they are afraid to speak of or think about.

You mean like You usually do with me?

Yes. It is a most effective means of teaching, for all teaching is really self-teaching. You cannot teach them anything, you can only point the direction, and suggest possible questions to consider and alternate answers. They must ultimately find the truth for themselves, or else they shall not benefit from it. If you simply tell them the truth, it will usually do them little good.

What about the koans and discussing them?

Yes. Like My parables, the koans you have been given can be very useful, if the person is somewhat advanced already.

Which of these methods is best to start with?

You shall know when the time is right. There is something which is very profitable and beneficial to most all of them, and it is a good starting point.

What is that?

Assisting them to feel better about themselves. This is a noble form of love, for it is a great need that man has and it is the best of pleasure.

Okay, Dad, how can I assist people to feel better about themselves? This sounds like an excellent first step for most in the teaching process.

First, you must understand about pleasure and help them to understand about pleasure. You must assist them to admit that they don't feel very good about themselves and that the reason is because of certain false beliefs that they hold about themselves.

You mean help them back toward a more natural outlook about themselves?

Yes. Feeling good about yourself is a very natural thing. If you didn't have any reasons to dislike yourself, then you'd naturally like yourself. And when you do like yourself, you will feel better about yourself. This also makes very fertile soil to plant the seeds of truth in, and establishes a good, healthy, loving relationship between you and the learner.

Sounds good. Why do so few of us feel really good about ourselves?

Feeling good about something is tied directly to liking it and enjoying it. You cannot feel good about camping if you do not enjoy it. Whenever you say <u>feeling good</u>, or the <u>good feeling</u>, what you are referring to is JOY. You have joy in the things that you allow yourself to EN-JOY.

So, few people feel good about themselves because few people enjoy themselves?

Right. And they don't allow themselves to enjoy themselves because they don't like themselves. You cannot enjoy what you don't like—it's impossible; they are opposites.

And why don't they like themselves?

They do not like themselves because of false beliefs about themselves.

Like what?

Mainly, they think that they are not very good.

Why is that a barrier?

You only like what you believe is good.

And since they believe that they are not very good, they don't like themselves very much?

Right. And since they don't like themselves very much, they won't allow themselves to enjoy themselves very much.

And when they don't enjoy themselves very much, they don't feel good about themselves. This is a long chain of effects!

Yes, and it's even longer. We shall discuss this later, however.

Okay. What is the core problem to overcome here?

The core is that most people think that they are not good. This is the real root cause of the greatest evils in the chain.

What is the worst symptom of this chain?

Since they think they are bad, they feel that others would not accept them. THEY wouldn't accept someone as bad as they believe that they are!

So they believe that they are unacceptable—and then what happens?

This is the start of the worst evil of mankind: phoniness.

When in a person's life do these things usually take place?

These changes usually take place in childhood. The effects may not be seen until later, yet the roots are strongly planted early.

What is the result of the false belief that I am bad and people won't accept me as I am?

The child begins to create a false image to show to others that he thinks they will accept. They start ACTING and being unnatural.

So that's why we start acting phony—we believe that no one will love us as we are because we think we are bad!

Right. And after years of wearing your masks, you forget how to take them off. You lose your most prized possession.

Which is?

Your SELF; that is, your integrity. And this makes you feel even worse about yourself—you dislike yourself and this reinforces your masks and phoniness. It's another vicious circle. There is a very terrible consequence of this vicious circle.

What is that?

It defeats the primary purpose of your being alive, and therefore cuts you off from true fulfillment.

You mean to be loved by God?

Yes. You see, your false image when loved doesn't receive any benefits. The real you, hiding inside of the closet of your mind, behind the masks and phony clown suits, never receives any love and starves for this true love. It feels unloved and unlovable. And this reinforces the false beliefs also.

I'm not real clear on why you can't receive any love when you're wearing masks and being phony or ACTING unnatural—not being your real self.

Okay, I'll give you an example. Let's say that you are the actor that played Gandhi in the movie. After the movie has run and many people have seen it, a man comes up to you on the street one day and says, "Oh, Gandhi! Man, I really dig your message of love and peace. I really admire and love you, man, and all that you stand for!" And then you say, "Excuse me, I'm not really Gandhi, I'm an ACTOR and that's just A ROLE I PLAY." Then the man is silent, so you say, "What do you think about me?" And he says, "NOTHING! I don't know YOU!"

I see! That's terrible! That would make me feel even worse.

Yes, even when someone does accept and admire this false image you have created and shown to them instead of your true self, it makes your true self feel worse and withdraw even further.

So most people withdraw deep into themselves, hiding, afraid of rejection, afraid of everything, not able to receive love, feeling lost and frightened and alone and forsaken by all.

Yes, and this is the state of most of the people's true inner self when they will come to you in the beginning. And they will not even believe these things about themselves. It's much like alcoholism; the alcoholic refuses to admit the truth to himself. Until he suspects that it might be true, he usually won't allow anyone to really assist him to a better mind about himself.

Yes, I know that just this same sequence of events happened to me—I experienced most everything that we spoke of. And then I made my commitment and You came and slowly and carefully drew the scared, innocent, ashamed child out of the closet of my personality; out into the light of truth and reason. Then You showed me this child's true beauty and value and power and glory. It was wonderful!

And before I came, would you have thought or admitted that these things were true?

No. I was the alcoholic. I didn't have a problem—or so I thought. I didn't think I was unhappy or unfulfilled—but then I had never really experienced these things in their true forms before, either. And I wouldn't have admitted that, either. I thought I knew what life was all about and I thought I was pretty happy. Man, what a crock of self-deception I laid on myself!

It's very common. And it is a true shame. Yet life is marvelous! There is help! There is something more!

Boy, do I know it. The difference between my old self, Mark—who still pops up occasionally—and Peniel, is like the difference between rapture and mere pleasure.

And you, Peniel, shall guide many from the dark recesses of quiet desperation out into the dazzling brilliance of truth and the bathing warmth of pure love. This I will allow you to do for Me, for I love you very much!

And I love You all that I can.

And one of the highest acts of love is to lead a person back to HIMSELF. For this, in essence, brings true life back to them! I shall assist you to bring others dead to the beauty and joy of living back to life and love and rapture. This is My will.

And mine. You're right, for if love takes care of needs and gives pleasure, this action, then, is one of the highest—for it is the most desperate need for many people and it will bring true joy and rapture where it could not exist before!

And almost everyone really wants to be their true self and stop acting phony and playing all the silly games with other people that they play. They want to be free. They want back the pure joy that they had as a child, which stemmed from their innocence and integrity and lack of false beliefs. It is not a treasure lost forever; it may be recovered. I have already taught you several ways that it can be done. Teach those that I send you this one thing first, and you will have done them and Me a great service!

I shall.

Most people are willing to stop lying to themselves. And when they become sincere about learning the truth, then they will be willing to open their minds and accept all the truth. They want to feel good about themselves, and love themselves again, and enjoy life truly. They shall learn—if they choose to. I have provided them a way now.

So why don't more people do this?

They are stopped by ignorance and fear.

What ignorance?

Most people know that the worst thing in the world is a phony—and since they know that no one likes a phony, they deny the truth to themselves. They convince themselves that: <u>I am really just as I seem to be. This is the real me—I'm not acting now—really—REALLY</u>!

And they accept this, don't they?

Yes, and then they become self-deceptive. This is a bad state to be in. It is the crime that the evil religious leaders of My time were guilty of. They had deceived themselves into believing that they were doing God's will; they dared to challenge Me, attempted to trip Me up and prove Me wrong and turn the crowds against Me.

And how did You defend Yourself?

I didn't have to defend Myself. I had the power that they didn't.

And what was that?

The TRUTH. And there is always great power in the truth. It matters little how they feel about you, if you speak the truth, the good ones will eventually accept you, for they love the truth!

I see. So I need not defend myself or give any justifications for my beliefs.

Not if they are true. Are they true?

Unless You are my imagination! But I don't think that I could have imagined all of these deep truths that You have told me. A lot of this is stuff that I never even considered or gave any thought to before.

Don't worry. I will defend you Myself. And woe to those who will reject you and fight to slander you because you believe the things I have told you.

I don't worry. I trust You and I know I love You and You love me. Reason itself will be the guide of those who have an open mind and read these things and really are seeking the truth. I haven't seen anything put down in these writings yet that is against reason and logic. I find most of it very reasonable and fairly simple to comprehend.

It is. When I was on earth, they expected I would only talk about religion and law and sins and politics. They had no idea that God was very simple and humble. They didn't expect that I would tell jokes and laugh and go to parties and have fun. They expected a very serious and stuffy Savior. I am not like that, as you well know.

Yeah. If You walked into work and everyone knew that You were <u>God</u> and You told a good funny joke, I think they would all be too scared to laugh!

Yes. But you would laugh, wouldn't you?

Sure, if the joke was funny.

All My jokes are funny!

Well, some of them just don't appeal to me very much.

I accept that.

You know that a lot of the people reading this are thinking, *Shocking! To think that Peniel proposes to talk with GOD as if He were a real person! The very idea!* I just know it. They think that You don't talk like a real person and that You never joke and You're always serious and stuff.

So, let them keep their misperceptions. Be glad that you know Me better.

I am.

Back to helping people. How can a person tell for sure if he really is his true self, or if he may be deceiving himself?

Okay, I'll explain how to tell. I know that this is going to hit some of the readers hard and I make no apologies; if you are deceiving yourself and aren't aware of it—it's good that you find this out even if it is a little painful.

Like Virgil, back home, before—he said that he was afraid that he might have lung cancer so mom suggested that he go to the doctor to get it checked out.

And what did Virgil say? Listen up reader; this may sound familiar to you!

He told mom, "Oh, I couldn't go to the doctor! I'm too afraid that they WILL tell me that it is cancer!"

And what happens if he doesn't go to the doctor, and it is cancer?

He has fixed himself so that he can't get the treatment the he really needs. He loses.

And if he doesn't go to the doctor to get checked and he really DOESN'T have cancer?

Then, he will never overcome his worry and be relieved that he doesn't have cancer. He has forced himself to have no chance to overcome his fear and worry. He loses again.

And this is the kind of corner many people will paint themselves into.

Okay, tell us how to tell to avoid that.

If you were your true self, how would you feel?

You would fully enjoy yourself and your life. As we discussed earlier, when you are your true self, you will love yourself. And when you love yourself, you will enjoy life fully.

To be a true success is to be your true self, nothing more. And if you were your true self, you would be completely satisfied with yourself. So here's the test—answer TRUTHFULLY this one question: Is there anything about yourself that you would like to have different or change in any way?

I see. If they were really their true self, they would answer, "No." And I don't know more than a couple of people who could honestly answer that question with a No.

Right. Most people would rather have a different I.Q., job, thoughts, habits, feelings, friends, home, position, family, spouse, abilities, control, looks, sexual attributes, et cetera.

If you were your true self, you'd be satisfied with all of these things just as they are.

Yes. It makes a good yardstick to check how far along toward perfection you have come. The closer to perfection you are, the more satisfied and in love with every aspect of your current life you will be. If you dislike a lot of the things about yourself or your situation, then you can greatly benefit from the truth.

And I'll bet there are still some people out there who will read this and even go to the lengths to make themselves believe that they wouldn't change anything about their self or life.

That's okay. If they're correct, then they're perfect and already have the truth. If they're deceiving themselves even to this point, they are as yet unwilling or unable to learn. Either way, they need not seek the truth.

I see. How does a person return to being his true self?

There are four main steps to take before you can once again become your true self and enjoy life fully. They are: acknowledge and accept that you are not yet perfect or your true self, identify the main areas where you are phony or unnatural, plan how to overcome your false beliefs and misconceptions—the root cause of all of these problems, and then TAKE ACTION. Don't plan forever, or else this will become a way to keep you from starting. Action is probably the key element. That is where the sincerity comes in. If a person isn't really sincere or is just playing the game of Help Me, I'm Lost, then they will not persevere in their actions; they will give up or make themselves quit or fail or lose interest.

So if a person follows these four basic steps, he may return to himself and once again enjoy the wonderful life that he could have.

Sure. It worked with you didn't it?

But what if they aren't sure of Your call or if they don't clearly hear You?

Then they have you. I will send them to you and I will guide them through you—if you choose to let Me work through you.

I do. So how do I assist people to understand all this?

Assist them as I did—through example. Let them come and experience you as you are and decide for themselves if the kind of joyous life you have is appealing to them or not. If they sincerely desire to have joy in life as you do, they will overcome their fear of you and eventually ask you to teach or guide them. Or, they may just want to ask you some questions.

That would be easy. My life already is so full of joy and love that I think it will be a good example of how their lives could be. I think this is a simple and marvelous idea.

Naturally. I'm a simply marvelous guy!

You sure are. I love You, sweet Father of mine. Teach me to better enjoy life and love so that I will be a good example for others to accept.

I am doing it even now! I love you.

CHAPTER 9
How To Be Your Natural Self

Me: Hello, sweet Jesus.

God: Hello, Peniel.

Well, I'm ready to learn about how people can once again become themselves.

Fine. This can be very useful for some of the readers. Yet it only tells what is done—not how.

Let's talk about the very first step. How does a person get started?

After he has proven himself sincere—you will show them how to prove their sincerity at the time—then they may start.

Let's say that a person has proven himself sincere to me; then what?

To get from here to there you must know two things.

What are they?

First, you must know where here is.

And second?

Second, you must know which direction will lead toward there.

Let's talk about the first step. What does here mean to a person seeking to become his true self again?

Here means his state—physically, mentally, personally, emotionally, and spiritually. Two things primarily determine it: attitude and beliefs.

What does there mean?

It means your true self with your true attitudes and beliefs intended for you, your perfect self—all that you can be.

How does a person go about getting from here to there?

He must first acknowledge and understand that he is not already there.

Then what?

Then he should get a good idea of how far he is away from there.

How is this determined? What question can they ask themselves to find out?

This question: Is there anything about your self, life, or situation that you would like to be different than it is now?

Only those who have already reached Nirvana or those who are not yet ready to learn will answer yes to that. Any of those would benefit from the training that we are dealing with. So, let's assume that the reader answers yes to this question.

Now that you have acknowledged that you are here, you must decide if you truly want to get to there, for it may be a long and hard trip. It is far better to not start this trip at all, than to start and fail, and refuse to finish.

You mean some people will be too scared or lazy to make the entire trip?

Yes, especially if it is a long trip for them. How do you get from here to there?

I guess I need a map.

Yes, a map could be useful. However, all you really need to start is a direction and a compass.

And Peniel will be the guide, so I guess for the person who is learning from me, I am the compass for him.

Right.

Okay, I get that. How do we determine which direction to take?

That's simple. Go the other way.

I don't get it.

Well, was this person ever there before?

Yes, when he was young he was a natural person—his true self—so he was there then.

And how did he get from there to here?

He accepted an act and false beliefs.

Yes. He chose the path of bad habits, misperceptions, and false beliefs.

So if we simply retraced his earlier steps in reverse, then we would be going from here back to there for him.

And will there be any way to tell if you are on the right path, going back the right direction?

We might just see some old familiar sites or landmarks he passed on the way here.

Very good. And what might some of these old familiar landmarks be?

The old landmarks would be old beliefs, memories, decisions, and things like that.

And do you have to follow the exact path back to get back to there?

No. But it might be a little easier that way because of its familiarity.

What do you need to insure your return trip?

I would say mainly the compass. As long as you keep going in the right direction, you'll get closer to there than you now are.

Good. What else do they need for the trip?

Perseverance.

And where will they get this?

If they will ask You for it, You will give it to them—if they will accept it from You.

This is true. And what about you as their guide? Will you leave them?

No, not unless they refuse to follow in the direction that I lead them. If they refuse to follow, and I am on my way to there, then they will be responsible for it.

Yes, Peniel. You understand your mission as a guide and teacher very well.

Now let's speak of your own journey.

Certainly.

Are you there for yourself?

Yes, but occasionally I leave for a while and walk a little way back toward here.

And when you do walk away, I may decide to send a person more advanced than yourself for you to learn from.

That would be wonderful.

But be cautious, for there will be some who will come to you and will have their own mind and desires at heart rather than your love and assistance. They will attempt to deceive you into believing that they are My missionaries to teach you. Yet you know well how to tell whether they are from Me or not, don't you?

Yes, You have taught me well. If they do not have pure love and truth as their companion and guide, they are not of You. If they offer beliefs that are not reasonable and do not agree with truth and love, then what they propose does not have to be accepted.

Very good—remember this for later when others attempt to lead you. You will be able to tell their motive by the fruits of their wisdom. And you know what I have taught you are the differences between a fool and a wise man and how to test them.

Yes, I remember.

I have no worry about you and your path, should you stray away and I send one to lead you back.

How shall another person decide if he should follow my guidance and instructions for him or not?

His heart will tell him, if he is attuned to hear its promptings. If he finds your teachings enlightening and appealing to him, he will be drawn to you. Then, when he meets you, he will decide to follow you based on his opinion about your personality, loving ability, and wisdom.

Then I don't think that I shall have any problem, once I can open up completely and show them my true self and my wants and passion to love You and teach others the truth.

Yes. Once you open up to a person and they allow you to become intimate with them, they will be taken in by the immense love and wisdom I have given you.

Thank You very much for these wonderful gifts.

You're welcome. You'll need them when you teach others.

For someone who decides to be led by me back to their true self, what tools will assist me to determine where they now are?

You can use several aids to determine what false beliefs, attitudes, and fears they currently have—such as the personality logbook and personality determination questionnaires, and the battery of tests.

What else?

You might decide to use the spiritual questions and answers to test them. This would also be a good test of their sincerity, for you know how people fight to not have to think about those things and find out what beliefs they hold inside themselves.

That could work out well.

And if someone reads this and decides that he wants to learn from you and cannot come to be with you yet, he can be tested with these things before he decides to come. After the questions, he may decide that it is too difficult for him or he doesn't really want to become his true self yet.

Yes, I see that this would be good.

Reader, if some of this appeals to you and you would like to find out for yourself, ask for the initial tests. I will probably give you just a few sample ones first to find out where I think you are and which direction I believe you should go. They will assist me to understand where you are and show me that you are sincere enough to have answered them. They are not easy questions, and I will be able to tell if you put much thought and effort into answering them from the insight that your answers contain. Please take me up on this offer if you are even a little curious. Just answering the initial questions may be very beneficial for you.

If they contact you, Peniel, you may use any sincerity test you want.

I think that clears up everything I wanted to know about it. How about if I put some sample spiritual questions after this conversation to give the reader an idea of what the tests are like?

Sure, that would be good. Put them on the next page after this talk.

Thank You, Dad, for being who You are and not what others think You are like! I like You very much as You really are! I love You.

And I appreciate all that you do for Me. I love you, dear Peniel.

Good-bye, sweet Jesus.

SOME SAMPLE QUESTIONS

1. What is your one wish in life? If you could get one thing, what would you wish for?
2. If you found out that you only had one week to live, what would you do? Include details.
3. What do you believe is your mission or purpose as an individual person in life?
4. Explain what heart means here: If you know a man's heart, then you know the man.
5. Why would a good God send any of His loved children to hell?
6. Where is the body of Jesus?
7. Can God make a weight so heavy that He can't lift it?
8. Why did Eve choose to partake of the forbidden fruit?
9. Why does God allow Satan to tempt us?
10. When is the soul put into a person?
11. What are the moralities of abortion?
12. What is your ultimate goal in life?
13. What is your greatest fear?
14. What do you think fear really is?
15. What one word description do you think best describes you? Why?
16. What is time and why is it there?
17. What denotes a sin?
18. Explain to me about the unforgivable sin.
19. Did demons have offspring by human women? If so, what were their offspring like?

20. What will the anti-Christ be like? What will he do and how will he do it?

21. What does Satan really want?

22. If Satan repented of his evil now, would God accept him back?

23. Explain the Trinity of God.

24. What was Jesus like as a child?

25. Why was the New Testament put together? Why did the assemblers do it?

26. What you think UFOs are and where are they from?

27. What did Mary and Joseph do with all of that gold, frankincense, and myrrh?

28. Did the boy Jesus ever make a mistake or act incorrectly?

29. Tell me about heaven: where will it be, where is it now, what will we do there, et cetera.

30. What happens to your soul after you die?

31. Where is the soul in your body?

32. Explain about Jesus' humanity and divinity.

33. Did Jesus ever get sick or catch a cold or anything like that?

34. Why did Jesus say: "You do not take the children's bread and throw it to the dogs"?

35. Did Jesus love the religious leaders of His time? Why did He speak as He did?

36. Who was Martin Luther?

37. What does the pope have as a position?

38. How does God feel about different denominations?

39. How does God feel about different religions?

40. WHO ARE YOU? (Not what are you, or details about you—WHO?)

CHAPTER 10

Why Do We Hurt The Ones We Love?

Me: God?

God: Yes, Peniel.

I would like to discuss something with You.

Okay, I always like to talk with you. What would you like to talk about?

I'm a little sad and mostly puzzled.

What are you sad about?

Well, I have been following the suggestions in one of Og Mandino's books and I am reading his "Scrolls of Success." This is coming along well. I'm in the second week of scroll II and I notice it helps me when loving others, but I still have trouble showing love to those really close to me. It sounds crazy, but I guess it's true that it's always easiest to hurt the ones you love the most.

It shouldn't be this way, but it is many times. You mean Gail and Summer, right?

Yeah. Why am I so obstinate in my refusal to practice what I preach? I find it pretty easy to be God with everyone else but them. Sometimes I make a little progress, but usually I am dissatisfied with how I love them.

Yes. It always seems easy to hurt the ones that are closest to you.

Why do we hurt the ones we love?

If you treated a friend like you occasionally treat Gail or Summer, what would they do?

Maybe tell me off or not come around me for a while. They might even dissolve our friendship, if I treated them badly enough.

So, does your fear of being rejected stop you from mistreating your friends?

Yeah, I guess it does—some. If I consider saying something sarcastic or doing something unloving, my fear of losing them as a friend checks me from doing it sometimes.

And is this good?

Yes. It keeps me from doing evil.

Is that good?

It's not bad.

Okay. Why don't you stop yourself in the same way with the ones you love the most?

Because I guess I'm not afraid of losing them. They're family and they have to accept me no matter what. Is that it?

Primarily. You either believe that they must accept you, or else you believe that they need you and can't get along without you. Either one of these beliefs can serve as a license to mistreat those who are close to you.

So I believe I can mistreat them without fear of retaliation. That's terrible!

Yes, it's bad, and most all people do this.

First of all, don't be so hard on yourself. You're doing very well so far. You're a very good husband and father; just stop and remember how you treated them two years ago, or take a good look at almost any other married man around you. You are a rare prize for both Gail and Summer now.

Yes, I have come a long way. I am better, but I want to be perfect—especially with them!

I know, and I admire your love of them. You do realize that sometimes it is a challenge to love them; I make it a challenge for you, so that your loving ability will be perfected all the sooner. It is My wish for you to become all that you can be as soon as you are willing to accept a new task.

Okay, I accept that; yet I know that my love for You, sweet Jesus, is primarily expressed to You through loving them.

Yes, and when you love them purely, you can love any purely, for I make it a challenge to love them.

I wish to be better at loving them. How can I improve myself in this area?

Continue to follow Me.

I will.

Perhaps your dissatisfaction with your own progress is unwarranted, or based on just a few isolated incidents. You realize that it often seems that normal behavior goes unnoticed, while some isolated incident of abnormal behavior receives conscious attention because of its distinction from the typical. It's like a kingdom where everything is made out of solid gold. It becomes so common as to be even unnoticeable in its preciousness. When something made of clay arrives, it's remarked about and stared at and focused upon by all. Let us examine what you believe to be some specific examples and perhaps we shall discover that this may be the case for you in your loving of your family.

Okay. I expected to be quite a bit different in my actions toward Gail when I returned from my latest trip, and I didn't notice quite the changes that I want to see.

Like what, specifically?

Well, such as the book that You guided me through on being more independent and in this way showing greater love to them. That enlightened me in some new ways as to how I was abusing Gail, treating her as if she were my servant and not my loved wife and equal.

And before you left, what did you tell her?

I told her that I might change some by the time that I returned. That I was going to do more for myself and rely less on her for things that I could do perfectly well myself—things that I was having her do out of my own laziness. That I was abusing the privileges of having a loving wife, and that I would stop.

And how have you been doing in this specific area?

Very good, I believe. It was mainly silly little things, like leaving my clothes laying around for her to pick up, or having her get my socks for me instead of getting them myself. I was acting helpless to get more attention from Gail because I wanted more love.

And how does Gail feel about the changes in you?

I don't know; I haven't asked her yet. I decided to give her some time to get used to the differences and then ask her for her opinion.

How do you think she feels about the changes you have made?

I think she is very pleased.

And do you think that this is good and real advancement?

Yes. I see; this area is much better. However, I think I have improved here at the cost of slipping back in another area.

And what is that?

I seem to have slipped in my normal feelings of enjoying their company and my feelings of love for them.

So, what are you saying?

I notice more problems in my everyday loving of them now that I have become more independent.

Excellent! I am very pleased!

What? You're pleased that I love them less in important ways?

No.

I don't understand, what do You mean? Explain why You are so pleased.

I am pleased that you are noticing more ways in which you do not love them in the way that you wish to.

Why? Isn't it bad to love someone less and treat them worse?

Yes, it's very bad.

So why are You so pleased?

You don't understand. You're not being any less loving than before. You're probably a little more loving than before.

How can that be? All that I see is how many little things that I could improve myself in!

I know, and that's what pleases Me so much!

What?

That you SEE! You are not less loving than before; you are actually a little better. However, because of your new commitments to be more independent, you can now see more clearly problem areas that you were BLIND to before. You can now SEE! And it pleases Me that your sight and clarity has been given to you in this area. Now you can work on these remaining problems. Before you committed yourself to independence, you were unable to see these particular areas.

You are little different than you were before, in your actions in question here, and now you see clearly what you are doing! It only seems to you that you are much less loving because of your new clarity.

I am glad that you have willingly received this wonderful gift from Me. It will greatly aid in your perfection of loving those closest to you, as is My wish for you for now. Do you understand all of this clearly now?

Yes, it's beautiful! I just didn't understand. I was starting to doubt if I was on the right path here or not, I saw so many problems that I thought I was causing.

And you <u>are</u> causing them. And you were doing the same things before I gave you your new eyes, only now you don't refuse to see it! So it only appears to you that you are worse. You are really better, only you see the bad within yourself that before went unnoticed.

And I guess that it's very important to see these things that are problems that we do out of habit that usually escape our attention, right?

It's extremely important! It's one of the main barriers that most people experience that brings their advancement to a screeching halt. It is probably the single most difficult type of barrier to be overcome: willful ignorance and self-induced blindness! This is the main reason why people who really want to advance stop advancing. It's impossible to work on a problem or barrier until you recognize it and identify it as a problem or a barrier! I am ecstatic that you have gained this new insight into your own actions and love. Don't see your noticing of further problems in any area as a step backwards or a failure. See it as a great victory over your worst enemies at this time: ignorance and self-deception.

So my clarity is a precious gift and it does not displease You that I do these things and notice these slight faults in my purity of love.

It displeases Me that you still have little faults in your purity of love. But it displeased Me more before, because not only did you do the same things, you did not even care about them or notice them. The evil that you did was evil only; it could not be used for any good or for your advancement. And evil that cannot be used for some improvement or good is far worse than evil that can be learned from.

Know this! All evil displeases Me very much, for I wish perfection. I made you perfect, and perfect is how I will you to be. Yet I am fully aware of your predicament, state, and problems. I am long-suffering and patient with all of you.

My main concern is to know that you are advancing, striving, loving, living fully, and enjoying—for I am your loving Father and I care much about all of you. When you do evil and it cannot be applied in any way to good or advancement because of your callousness or self-deception—as was the case for you—that is a great sin. It is like the useless shedding of innocent blood for sport—what good will come from it? It displeases Me and distresses My heart!

Oh, sweet Lord. I am deeply sorry for my callousness before, and I repent of all of these evils that I did without even being consciously aware of them. Please help me and have mercy on me and my stupidity, human foolishness, and self-deception. I swear to You that I shall never again be as I was. Assist me to make the commitments necessary to see clearly my faults and evil, and I shall willingly accept Your sweet gifts and apply them most liberally in my life, for I wish only to be what You desire of me and all that You desire of me. If being my true perfect self is Your desire, than let that be my will.

I am very moved by your love and desires, Peniel. You are a rare treasure for Me and I love you very much. Receive My blessing and know that indeed I shall show you all things necessary for your advancement and perfection. I love you.

And I love You. I shall treasure this new clarity about this aspect of my life, like I treasure all of the clarity You have given me in other areas like it. Thank You for this wonderful gift; I shall appreciate it from now on. When I see a fault in my loving and habits, rather than being displeased with myself and feel guilty, I shall be urged to immediately change my actions and habits and make immediate restitution for my error. I shall see each fall as a rare opportunity to advance, improve, and come one precious step closer to complete Nirvana and perfection so I may be infinitely pleasing and acceptable as an offering to You when it is time.

And understand further that clarity is vital to your mission in life. It is of utmost importance to have true clarity when you teach, guide, command, and rule, for how can you explain and make acceptable anything that you are unclear on yourself? Now that you have perfect clarity in this area, you may easily assist anyone else who sincerely seeks to learn about this aspect.

This area is one of the major stumbling stones for many whom I will send to you for your instructions and guidance. It is very important to your mission and full service to Me as I have destined it for you, so it is greatly important for you to have learned and fully grasped.

I am celebrating because you have fully overcome one of the biggest barriers to your perfection that remained—your ability to guide others unerringly! Great is My joy in you and for you. Now we have overcome an obstacle that seemed insurmountable before. I have worked long to bring you to this doorstep. Now you shall make great improvements quickly, for now your eyes are open to it; I am overjoyed at this great victory for us!

I didn't realize that this was of such great significance. I thought that we were dealing with little problems and minor discrepancies.

Comparatively, we are. We're not dealing with giant sins or earth-shaking problems. I realize that they seem small compared to the earlier obstacles that you have overcome with My assistance. Yet consider this: if all that remains between you and perfection is one small obstacle, and this small obstacle is of no great relevance compared to earlier ones, it is the BIGGEST obstacle you have left. And as such, overcoming it is a time for great rejoicing. I am so pleased for you, for I know what is immediately ahead for you, if you choose it!

Well, I'm getting caught up in Your contagious enthusiasm! I think I'll quit writing and go kiss and love my wife some. Thanks for the gifts and showing me more clearly that they are of more significance than I thought!

★★★

Well, how did you find your wife? Was she receptive to your enthusiastic love?

No, she was like a cold fish. I really wanted to share my joy with her, but she was busy reading and dealing with matters of consequence—if You understand what I mean.

Yes. Didn't I say that sometimes I make it difficult for you to love her?

Yes, and I guess this was one of those times.

Do you understand that I don't do this so that it is difficult for you to love her, for that is not My wish; I do it because it is ultimately best for you, for it gives you the opportunity to love her even though she is not willing and receptive. It is difficult for you, so if you can succeed in loving her purely when it is extremely difficult, then at any other time it will be extremely easy.

Yes. I clearly understand that and I appreciate that You care about my quick advancement enough to send me tests such as this. I know that You do this out of love for me and that it is for my perfection. I used to resent You for doing this, and I resented Gail or Summer for their refusal to receive my intense love. Now I see that what I perceived as a difficulty before is really a blessing in disguise.

Always remember that ALL things work for the good of those whom I love and are in My favor! If you had no choice in it, then I chose or influenced it for you, Peniel, and I will only do what is good and best for you! And if you do not see it as good, it is just another of your misperceptions. See the good behind all things that I send you. You are in My favor!

I shall.

Shall we now talk more in general terms about why man hurts the ones he loves so that I will gain deeper insight now that I am more receptive to this subject?

Yes. Why do we usually treat our friends with more respect than we do our family?

Two reasons: fear and contempt.

Why fear?

As we said, you fear that your friends will reject you, and you mistakenly believe that your family must accept you and won't reject you.

You did know that this is a false belief, right?

Yeah. I know that your family can reject you if they choose to, but that it is one of those false social taboos. And because it is, most families won't reject you until they can't stand it any more. Is this why oftentimes separations and family problems are so intense and blown out of proportion when they finally do come to a head?

Yes. People keep the resentments inside because of these socials taboos and the anger builds until some little straw breaks the camel's back. Then they explode over some seemingly insignificant thing.

I see. This explains a lot of things about trouble in relationships that I have seen before.

In truth, your family is neither really in need or dependent upon you. You sometimes make them believe that they are, because you are looking for open doors to treat them any way you want to, including hurting them.

Why do we do this if we really love them?

You do this because of more false beliefs. Many people believe that if their loved ones knew that they were really independent, they wouldn't put up with some of the things you might pull. A person thinks that it is restricting to his freedom for his loved ones to act as they choose if they are too independent of them.

They also attempt to justify their beliefs by saying that it is good that their loved ones are dependent on them, because that stabilizes the relationship. This is a crock, and if examined in truth for a moment, you will see this.

Love is not increased with dependency; love is strangled by dependency. When you love something, and you fear that you might lose it, uncage it and set it free. If it remains with you of its own free will, rejoice, for it truly loves you and is yours forever—you need not strangle it with restriction ever again for fear that it will leave you. If, however, it leaves you when you release it, rejoice still, for it was not really yours—you have spared yourself the cruel punishment of love turned to hatred of you for imprisoning it.

When love is imprisoned behind dependency and restrictions, it will change and sour and turn against you. It will seek the opportunity to hurt you, for it has turned to anger and hatred. You will pay the dear price for injustice to what was once love—rejection, and the punishment and guilt of not knowing where you went wrong! It matters not whether it truly was love originally or not, if caged it would go against you in time no matter which way it started.

I see. So if I wish to be perfect, I should encourage the independence of those that I love.

Yes, for love does not seek to make its object dependent upon it, rather it seeks to free its object so that its object may have greater freedom and ability to love in return. No one wishes to be caged or restricted. All wish to be freed and given more power.

I see. I shall remember this important lesson and teach it to others who seek truth sincerely.

Good.

What about the other reason why we treat friends with more respect than loved ones occasionally? How does contempt fit in here?

Someone once said that familiarity breeds contempt. This is not true, yet it seems to be this way in most cases.

Why?

Just like in Peniel's Ode *(see appendix),* you take things for granted. You stop appreciating the true beauty and value of things because they become commonplace to you. Most people mistakenly believe that true beauty and value are closely tied to rarity. This seems to be true, but it is this way only because man has accepted this false belief. You believe that a diamond is very beautiful and valuable because of its rarity, yet a common gnat you don't appreciate or value at all. Who sees the beauty in a gnat? The main reason few see the gnat's beauty is because I have been very generous in dispersing gnats. It is not My fault that man refuses to see the value and beauty of the gnat. It is a marvelous creation—it is alive and moves and flies and breathes and grows and eats and reproduces; it has a life and serves an important purpose in the overall scheme of nature's insects. Yet who is it that truly appreciates the lowly gnat only because it is not rare? There are other, less beautiful, creatures that man values and studies and preserves because they are very rare. But rarity, of itself, does not improve a thing's beauty, good, or value—although this is the commonly held belief among men.

I see Your point. We even do this with people—Your greatest miracle and the most beautiful and important creature that exists. We devalue their true beauty and importance simply because there are so many and they are common. If we were removed from all these things for a long time and weren't taught all of these common misperceptions, then we would have a truer appreciation of the inherent beauty and good and value of all things.

I thank You for where You have taken me. What else may I learn about this subject? What can a person do to best obtain once again the appreciation for the good and beauty and value in something—especially someone they love?

As with most everything else in a person's journey, this is tied to returning to your natural self. The major barriers to overcome are more false beliefs. Once you overcome them, you will have clarity of sight—it is sometimes called insight. This clarity is largely responsible for success, definiteness of purpose, and the further purification of love and self. Once a person has and accepts clarity, they may advance on to power.

Remember, when I came, I came to testify to the truth. This testifying to the truth—as is your mission also—is nothing other than the restoring of clarity for those who will accept clarity. The truth awaits all who will see it. The largest barrier between people and goodness and perfection is that they are not yet free. This is either because they do not yet have the truth because they have not yet sought it, or, if they have sought it and not yet found it, it is not because it is hidden, IT IS BECAUSE THEY CANNOT ACCEPT OR RECOGNIZE IT. THIS BECAUSE THEY DO NOT YET HAVE CLARITY!

Your mission is very important because it will restore the very ability that many are lacking for their further advancement in the spirit and mission and life. Understand and appreciate the importance of your task and mission in life.

I do, sweet Dad; thank You for selecting me for this noble purpose. I shall, with Your assistance, be the best teacher and guide to perfection that I may be. I shall do everything in my power to assist those sincere truth-seekers that You send to me to learn all that they wish to learn. I offer You all things for all good always and in all ways. I love You.

And I love you.

CHAPTER 11

What Man Fears Most

Me: I love You, sweet Jesus.

God: I love you too, Peniel.

I find that it will be kinda strange when my time finally comes and I openly speak with others about You and my conversations with You.

This comes from your speaking with Shiroda at work, doesn't it?

Yes. He seems pretty typical of people I meet, and I think his reactions are a pretty good indication of how the majority of people will take Peniel. I mentioned to him about this book that I was in the process of writing and what it was.

And how did he respond to the idea that you were writing a book about the conversations that you casually have with the Infinite Being and Creator of all things?

About like most everyone will probably take it. I think that if he didn't already know me pretty well that he would have had serious doubts about my sanity. I guess I would feel the same way if someone reported such things to me before I became enlightened and learned the truth.

And how did <u>you</u> feel?

I didn't really feel much. I had expected him to take it like he did. He's kinda quiet and reserved anyway. I sensed that it was a difficult thing for him; I can imagine how it must seem to him since he is little aware of my inner life and walk with You. I guess this is how it will probably be with most people for me in the future. AND I am sure that there are those out there like I was many years ago; people who have a desperate desire to find the truth and purpose and meaning in life. People who are looking for something to help make some sense out of what seems like a senseless world.

I know that there are many people like this out there who also possess the required sincerity to do whatever is needed to find the real truth and their mission in life. I know that for many years I would have given anything to have been able to have a guide or teacher to assist me along the path that I had chosen in hopes of loving and following You more closely. I was looking for someone just exactly like You have since made me. I'm very glad for all that You have done for me. I hope that there are many out there like I was who are sincerely looking for all of the truth, not just the parts of it that appeal to their desires.

You mean people COMMITTED to the truth, right?

Right. I hope to train those special twelve that You have told me about soon. It will be great to have the assistance of some enlightened brothers and/or sisters in Christ with the same goal and purpose in mind as myself to assist me in the noble task You will give us.

They will come in time. Perhaps some of them shall read this work and I shall tell them through it that their time to train and love Me has come.

That would be great. I've got so many plans for such wonderful programs for the future that You have laid out for me. I know that with Your assistance and the dedication and energy that You have given me—along with the assistance of others devoted to loving God through loving their fellow man—we can all make this world a much better place. Or, at least we can touch the hearts and minds of those whom You intend for us to touch, and do Your work in this way.

All things will come in time. Perhaps this book will start things rolling. If not, give it to those who you think may be ready to learn. I realize how eager you are to start teaching others and doing the work that I have told you about for Me. And you're right, many will not understand. Yet your love will melt all hearts like the sun's rays that soften even the coldest clay. If your love is pure and your motives are clear and good, and you continue to follow Me, all things will follow as I have destined them. I Myself will be your strength and shield. I do not say that the way will be easy, yet I do offer you the opportunity to daily pick up your cross and follow in My footsteps. My work will be your work and the work of those that you will train and accept into your group. I shall assist you to do great things—all that is required from you is everything.

And You know well that I give You my all.

Now, back to how people will respond to me. I think most of the people that will meet me when it is my time and yet do not know anything about me will respond in the same ways.

And how is that?

With fear and uncertainty.

Yes. It's hard for them to conceive of someone like you because of their commonly held false beliefs. You will be an oddity to many. Yet, it is for the few that I have sent you to teach. It was the same for Me. There may be great novelty in being what you will be, yet I know that you feel as I do about that carnival atmosphere: sincerity is best—and keeping a good sense of humor, and a light and enjoyable personality.

Well, it's the choice of others as to how they will respond to me and what I represent.

And what do you represent?

Hmmm. I guess I could sum it up best by saying I am a representative of Love, Truth and Joy.

You mean that you are a representative of Mine.

Yes. And if I say, "Hello, Mr. Ginsberg. I represent the Infinite Intelligence and Creator of the entire Universe. I have come here today to tell you THE TRUTH so that you can be truly free and fully enjoy life and know the secrets of life and the universe. Now here is my brochure; as you see, we have many programs and seminars on just about every aspect of life. Here's the 'How To Achieve All Of Your Goals' training that I am sure that you will be interested in. And of course I offer a complete line of Improvement Training Seminars and training courses in enjoying life, finding fulfillment, and the same old stuff that others have always been promising and not delivering. Well, I've gotta be going. Feel free to look over our brochures and contact us if and when you feel that you sincerely need some meaning and joy in life. Thanks for your time, and remember: the One I represent—God—loves you."

Sounds pretty good to Me.

You gotta be kidding.

Well, it might get a good laugh. And if you came as Peniel and allowed them a question and answer period, it would probably be very convincing. Many people are desperately seeking THE TRUTH, but they keep this to themselves. The best thing about your services is your prices! It is not rare that a person comes and wants to show you a brochure on their services and goods, but when they look and find that all of the goods and all of the services are provided absolutely free, that might turn some heads. Who wouldn't give you a fair hearing even if it does sound kinda crazy to them? They may be missing out on the chance of a lifetime—a chance that I Myself have set up and destined for them.

I have invested a great deal in preparing and training you, and giving you the wisdom that you now possess. I shall not have it wasted or squandered on those who will not benefit seriously from it. You do not cast pearls before the swine to be trampled in the mud.

Yeah, but I'm not too sure about the presentation of all of it.

Don't worry; leave the presentation in My hands. I will arrange everything as I have done before, and you will again see everything fall into place.

And I hope that You consider the needs of my family and those whom You will entrust in my care. We gotta eat, ya' know.

Yes. I will take good care of you. Perhaps the proceeds from this book will set you up nicely.

Right. I'm sure it will be a billion-seller. There ought to be at least that many sincere people around. (Laughs)

Some will understand your mission and be moved to assist you in whatever way they will. Do not worry; I'm a great financier and I will free you to do your job through other's support. You won't have to beg or sell your services, even though they are of great value. It would devalue the good and merit to ever charge for these things—freely I have given to you and freely shall you give to any that will receive these things. This is My way.

Those who truly follow Me do not continuously request support from those who love them. If your mission is needed and you are tied up in teaching, I will give others the benefit of having them assist you in your work in the way I direct them to. Never ask for anything from another other than love, loyalty, service, respect, and sincerity. And never demand these things—rather let your very being silently command and request these things. Remember, you are a free being also. I shall not force you to receive the abuse of others.

I suggest that if their abuse is unwarranted or unreasonable according to love, that you not allow them to continue to abuse you—for you know that I shall deal harshly with them for their unfair treatment of you. Rather, lovingly allow them to believe their own righteousness and remove yourself from their presence—for their benefit, not your fear or dislike of abuse. I know that there is almost no fear in you and I know how you would be willing to die for Me. I understand this.

Love all those who come to you, even though your love may demand that you treat them in a way that others view as unloving. Do not be concerned over what others tell you that you should or should not do—although keep an open mind and ear, for I may send word to you through others. I Myself loved the religious leaders of My time, yet because few people understand the true motives and workings of pure and intense love, few understood that My words and attitudes and action towards those evil men was the most loving thing that I could have done for them.

You shall probably be received in a similar way sometimes. Know that if another persecutes you because of your faith in yourself and Me, they did the same to Me. Rejoice that I find you worthy to hang on the cross of others' distrust and persecution beside Me.

I can imagine the way that my family will probably respond to all of this. Mike will be full of good advice, Billy will try to dissuade me from this career of loving others and teaching the truth, Cathy will probably have a hard time understanding all of it, Angela will be Angela, and Anita will think that finally the mystic Mark has arrived. Dianne still won't know me—none of them will. How will they ever survive the new me? I know that it will be difficult for all of them—I understand their feelings even before they have them. Gail and I have already talked about all of this because I wanted her to be prepared for the reception that we may get.

Yes, they all think that they know Mark pretty well. Yet, of your interior life I have only given them brief glimpses, and those sometimes didn't show you in a favorable light. Never mind; what will come will come. They are the ones responsible for their own feelings and attitudes toward you, remember this. Be grateful that I have given you the mother that I have given you. She is a rare prize because of her loving ability.

Yes, thank God for good ol' mom. She's the only one that will probably understand me. Yet even she may have a little trouble accepting Peniel.

Perhaps not. Peniel is not so different from Mark, just more good and loving. I really don't think that any of your family will fail to accept you after they come to know the real you better. After all, I have done a great job on you—you are a great guy.

Thanks. I will trust You. You know that it doesn't really matter to me whether they reject me or love me. I understand that they're only human. I just don't want them getting the wrong ideas about their little brother. Oh, well, it's all in Your capable hands and the decision will be theirs, not mine. I will love and appreciate their decision no matter what it is.

Remember, I went back to My own hometown and revealed My true self to them, and they ran Me out of town on a rail—so to speak.

Yeah, I remember. I'm glad that I don't have to please anyone but You.

When others do openly criticize you, how shall you receive their criticism?

As You have taught me to.

And how is that?

If they criticize me, I shall love them and receive it with joy. And I shall listen carefully to their harsh words, their anger, or whatever else they express to me.

Why will you be pleased when others criticize you?

Because either their criticism is true, or else it is unfounded and unreasonable.

And if their criticism is true?

Then You have sent them to me to assist in my advancement and perfection, and this will please me. I shall have the rare opportunity to note a fault in myself and overcome a new barrier I was as yet unaware of. This will please me.

And if their criticism is totally unreasonable, improper, or unfounded?

Then I will know that their criticism is unfounded and is stemming from their disapproval, hatred, anger, jealousy, or other negative feeling toward me. These are the things that You Yourself had to endure. I shall count myself blessed to be able to suffer some of the same injustice that my loving Savior endured, and I shall understand that it is also a test of my courage and purity of love. If I pass this test, my reward for suffering this unjust act in silence shall be wonderful.

I welcome the few opportunities that You do allow me to suffer some injustice at the hands of others. Most people I have encountered so far are good, loving people at heart. I believe all people are. I don't think that this shall be a big problem for me, even though I realize that it shall probably come in time.

And how shall you distinguish between the founded criticism and the unjust criticism?

As always, truth, reason, and love shall be my companions. They shall show me which is founded and which is unfounded. If the person has gripes based on reason or the true ways of love, I shall hear him out and learn from him. If he is only coming from some belief that he holds dear according to his interpretation of scripture or the like—a belief that is obviously contrary to the ways of love and reason—I shall understand him and pray for him.

Anything else?

Yes. Whether their criticism is good or not, I shall admire their courage for having brought it to my personal attention. I realize that because of my zeal in teaching, I sometimes come off as quite overbearing. I do not wish it to be this way, and yet it is. It usually creates an attitude of uneasiness or fear in most of those that I speak with about matters of relevance. Many of them say that they really wish to find the truth, yet when you hold the reasonable truth up against their dearly held false beliefs, they sing a different tune. Then they throw reason out the door and resort back to that "Well, these are mysteries that man cannot fathom" garbage because they have this strong need to be RIGHT rather than to find the truth. Thank God not all of them are like this.

I know that a lot of them get the impression that I am trying to prove them wrong at every turn. What I really do is to bring their false beliefs out into the light of reason and love, for them to take a closer look at. They usually flee in terror because of their fear of having to change or their fear of being WRONG! I don't give a rat whether they are right or wrong or what, I only care that they find the truth if they are sincerely looking for it.

And do you understand their fear?

Sure. I ought to understand it, it ruled my life for a long time while I was seeking the truth in other ways. I know that their own insecurity and lack of personal integrity is at the root of their fear of me and what I represent.

And what do you represent to them?

The TRUTH. The simple, reasonable, accessible truth that they are scared to death of confronting.

Why are they afraid of confronting the simple truth?

Because the truth doesn't pull any punches. The truth reveals all of those things within us that most of us are not yet ready to face. The truth reveals our own falsity and phoniness. It reveals our masks and games and—worst of all—our dearly held false beliefs.

Why do they fear seeing these false beliefs revealed?

Because they know that in the light of reason and the warmth of love these false beasts will shrink and fade because they cannot be defended with reason.

And why do they fear losing these closely held false beliefs?

Because, for most of them, that is all that they have left and they really don't trust that there are better replacements for them. They fear having to really change themselves or their lives. They fear a real commitment.

And now let us talk of their greatest fear. A fear so terrible that most of mankind rarely—if ever—is willing to seriously consider it and its implications.

What is man's greatest fear?

That there is no God! Because if there is no God, there is no reason or purpose for life. They are just an accident—a fluke of nature. They shall live and die, and it will all have been in vain and had no purpose. This is a universe of non-sense if you accept this fear. Many have been compelled to believe that I AM, not because of the reasonableness of My existence, but because of their greatest fear—that GOD IS DEAD or has never really been.

You're right. That is terrifying to even consider. Thank God I know the reasonableness of why You must be, along with my own personal experience.

And what do you think that man fears most after this fear?

I don't know, what?

That I DO exist, and that I am just as they have heard that I am.

Why would they fear that? If their greatest fear is that You don't exist, I would think that they would be relieved to think that You do exist. Why do they fear this?

Because of their false beliefs. They fear that if I do exist and I am like they believe I am, they will be unacceptable to Me. They fear that I shall reject them. They fear that they won't make it at judgment. They fear that they can't be forgiven. They fear just about everything that deals with Me, My dealings, and My very existence or non-existence. Why do you think that so few actively pursue the truth about Me sincerely like you did? What else in life is even remotely important compared to whether I AM or not? And if I AM, what is really important compared to what I really want of you, why I have created you, and what I request of you.

You would think that the majority of the people would devote the majority of their time to finding and teaching the answers to these most important of all questions. Yet how many do you know that will even sincerely listen to these things being discussed for very long? Oh, they are curious and like to inject their own two-cents worth of beliefs when they can, but when the truth comes out and one of their dearly-held false beliefs comes under fire, what do most of them do?

Run for the hills. I have seen it many times. And I know that there must be some sincere people out there.

Where are you, you that are sincere and seeking the truth, not just the parts of it that appeals to you? I don't force anything. I only propose many relevant questions and then assist you to discover the reasonable truths for yourself—if you are not too afraid!

Come, I await your sincerity; it will be refreshing like a breath of clean air among all of this pollution of insincerity. I anxiously await you. I know that you have fears and I shall give you relief, if that is what you seek. Come to me and tell me what you seek. I shall grant it, if it is within my power. I love you, dear reader, whoever you are.

Teach them, Peniel. Help them to see that I am a great guy and I am love itself. Teach them all that means. Teach them all of the things that they wish to know; I make you their boundless resource of simple, reasonable wisdom.

There is little that is truly beyond man's ability to comprehend. Many things like this get proposed simply because people refuse to accept the responsibility for having learned the truth. They mistakenly believe that their ignorance is a better state to remain in, so they say, "Who can fathom such deep mysteries of God? It is not for man to know!"

And I ask, "Who has set you up as judge of what I shall be willing to reveal. I am not complicated or deep. I am very simple and comprehensible. It is man who has invented much of these fantasies about what cannot be known."

Readers, if you fear that I don't exist, think again. If you fear that I will not love you, realize that I will. If you fear that I don't care, know that My love of you is infinite. If you fear that I will not forgive your offenses, know that there is no sin that is stronger than My love.

Why do you continually refuse to enjoy the pleasure and gifts that I send to you all the time? Why do you continually refuse to accept Me as I am? I love you, care for you, and wish to serve you. I will take care of all of your needs, and give you all the pleasure that you will receive from Me. You are so obstinate! I know well your problems and hopes and fears. Please allow Me the opportunity to bring you back to the truth. This is all that I ask of you. I love you, always and in all ways. Let Me love you!

Beautiful! You say things wonderfully even though filtered through my mind!

(Laughs loudly!) You are a real treasure, Peniel. Share My joy with Me over you!

(We paused while we shared a beautiful experience together as we embraced—I wish you could have felt this, it would have blown you away!)

You see, Peniel, even now there are many reading this and thinking, *He's loony. God doesn't embrace us or laugh or have a good time!*

Oh, My poor misguided children; who has taught you this? Do you still misunderstand Me so much even after reading all that I have already revealed in this work? What father does not wish to share the joy of mutual love with his beloved child with a hug and a kiss? Why do you think such thoughts as are now in your mind? Do you really know Me so well as to be able to judge whether I will do these things? Do you not realize that I am a real person just like you?

I am a very good person, too. I am like the most loving and fun person that you ever met, only better and more loving and more fun! Who do you think is the creator of joy? I am joy itself! I fully enjoy

Myself; why will you not accept this? Can you accept, at least, that I may be a little different than you believe that I am? I hope so, for your own sake. If you think that I am a stuffy, always serious, lightning bolt-hurler, I pity you. Know Me as I truly am!

Teach them about Me, Peniel. They need you to reveal the truth to them, since they won't listen to Me!

I shall teach them all that You wish for me to, sweet Lord. Just send them to me and give them an open mind and true sincerity.

I shall. Peniel.

I love You very much, Dad.

And I love all of you.

CHAPTER 12
Joy And Suffering

God: I love you.

Me: And I love You also, Father.

Today we will talk about joy and suffering.

Wonderful. Let's speak of joy first. What is joy?

Joy is the natural, energetic, positive experiencing of life and aliveness that each person was destined to experience normally.

Where does joy come from?

Joy comes from Me. I Myself am joy. In essence, to experience joy is to experience that part of Me that gives you your life. Whenever you touch that aliveness within yourself that makes you experience joy, you touch the God within yourself. When you feel joy, you are in touch with Me. I intended for all of mankind to have a continuous experiencing of this union between us, and the Fall has infected your ability to experience it normally. There was only joy in Eden; there was no suffering at all. Man was fully and continuously in touch with joy, for man was fully and continuously in touch with Me.

You mean that if I allow myself to take joy in smelling a flower or watching a child play, I am getting in touch with You inside of me?

Yes, for these things are reflections of the goodness and inherent pleasure in all of life. These are merely reflections of Me, for I am all-good and all that is. Whenever a person sees the good in anything, then, and only then, can he enjoy it. As we have said before, only that which is believed to be good may be enjoyed. And whenever a person sees the good in anything and allows himself to enjoy that good, it is none other that a reflection of Me that is the good being enjoyed. Do you understand?

Yes. Enjoyment is really touching life intimately, and You are that life that we touch intimately. To touch You is to experience joy, for You are joy itself.

Very good. I am the one who put the fragrance in the flower. To experience joy is to experience the wonderful mystery of life and self. In those moments when you are in ecstasy, you have come close to My presence; being in My presence is the source of joy.

Some things seem to always bring me joy—like watching Summer play.

This is because you have learned and made a habit of appreciating the beauty and goodness of an innocent child at play. It reminds you of your own innocent time; that was a time of joy for most children. These are the times you recall, the times when you were still your natural self and you still had your precious gifts of innocence, purity, and integrity.

Why do most of us become so callused when we grow up?

Several reasons. It can be summed up like this: you lose your vision of what is truly essential in life.

And what is truly essential?

I am.

So, all that we really need is You?

Certainly; if you have Me, you have everything—you lack nothing.

But aren't You in everything?

Yes.

So, do we need everything?

No. You are thinking of the various forms that I take, not the true essence of Me. It's like a can of fruit; which is essential, the container or the fruit?

The fruit. But in many cases the container may be useful and beautiful.

Yes. The container should be respected in its own right, yet you wouldn't throw away the fruit and eat the can.

I see.

And what is the essence of life itself?

Love; that is, You are.

And what is the essence of a human being? Are their looks or is their body the essential part?

No, it is their personality—their soul—that is truly essential about a person. All of the rest is just container and tools for use by their essence. It's like art: it is not the canvas and the paint that is the essence of the painting, but rather the image that the artist has created with this medium. This projection of the artist's thought and conception, which is the painting, is the creation that comes through the container of the canvas and the paint.

That is beautiful. And just as you have described, I am the artist and man is My painting. The canvas is his body, the paint is his appearance, and the image created through this medium is the personality. This is a pretty good analogy. And My art is all of all. It is rock and cloud and mountain and wind. My easel is the earth itself. My background is the universe. And My paint is life! My finest self-portrait is you: man.

Superb. But sometimes we don't see or appreciate the beauty! We trample the flowers under foot; we hurry off to work and don't see the miraculous sunrise. We watch TV instead of playing with our kids. No wonder man is so unhappy. We don't allow ourselves to enjoy any of life's greatest treasures.

And this is what I have said. You have lost your vision of what is essential in life. You no longer remember that I am an artist and that My work is superb and beautiful. You do not appreciate it because you whiz by at 55 miles an hour because you're late for work again.

And this is the premise behind Peniel's G.G.G. Koan. *(See Appendices.)*

Yes. It is a shame that innocence is so fragile and easily traded away.

Does innocence give that special vision that the fool in the cave had?

No. This vision is the natural vision. However, the loss of innocence is responsible for the loss of childlike vision also.

What is mainly needed to return to the childlike vision?

A return to innocence.

But is that possible?

With Me, all things are possible. If you really seek Me out and are sincere in your wish to return to innocence, I will return your personal integrity. Your innocence is a natural result of true personal integrity.

And how shall we reacquire our innocence?

You will receive Me, and I will restore it to you Myself. After I restore your innocence to you, all things necessary will follow naturally, so long as you continue to follow Me.

You mean, "Seek ye first the kingdom of God, and all things will be added to you"?

That's the essential idea.

Is this what is really essential in life—seeking God?

No. What is essential in life is not <u>seeking</u> Me, it is <u>having</u> Me. It is just a necessary and important step for most adults to seek Me first, for they have traded Me away for other things. I am the true possession of all natural children until they no longer accept Me, or until they lose Me or trade Me away. This is why they are so happy and content. And then they trade Me away. This usually happens to most persons before they reach adult life, hence the desperate need to return to their natural self and to once again claim their most prized possession—Me.

But what about seeking?

Well, you shouldn't have to seek Me—just My kingdom.

And where is Your kingdom?

Within each of you is the kingdom of God.

Since it is within us, how do we find it?

You can't find it. It is not lost.

Well then, how do we learn to recognize Your kingdom within us, and appreciate it and derive the benefits it is supposed to bring to us?

By following Me.

Where will You lead us?

Back to yourself. Back to personal integrity. Back to purity of intention. Back to joy in life. Back to Me.

So, to see You as the essence within the various forms You take, to see the good that is You, to appreciate this joy and allow it to affect us—this is JOY.

Exactly. To touch Me and know Me as I really am is to experience joy.

Does this mean that those people who continually refuse to enjoy any part of life are refusing to see You?

Yes.

And what happens when a person is not seeing or touching You through his own choice?

He experiences suffering and despair. And these are merely the lack or absence of joy and hope. If they continually refuse to see the good within anything, then the two greatest fears of man will come upon them.

You mean the fear that there is no God, and the fear that there is a God and that they are not pleasing to Him?

Yes. These false beliefs create the suffering and despair.

Let us speak of suffering now. What is suffering?

Suffering is the state of mind where I am not seen, touched, or experienced in any way. This is the mental state of those poor souls who will reside in hell for all eternity.

Can You give me an example of suffering that is not so intense?

Sure. If a situation occurs in which you cannot or will not see any good, then you experience suffering. If you cannot see any good, then you cannot experience any joy, for joy is the touching of the good that is seen. Since there is an absence of joy, suffering is the result. Basically, suffering is a result of being separated from Me. To not experience Me is to endure suffering. This is because I am the good and joy of life.

So our inability or refusal to experience You in a thing, place, person or whatever is why we suffer?

Exactly. Give Me an example, since you are having trouble understanding, and I shall demonstrate. Pick an example that you don't think fits in with My definition.

Okay. A small child has muscular dystrophy and will die within the next year. Surly the suffering that this child endures isn't caused by not seeing You.

It is. First, let's clear up a few false beliefs that I see you have.

Okay, shoot.

Could a child be in the situation that you are describing and experience quite a bit of joy?

Yes, I guess some could. But I'm sure that the vast majority of them suffer greatly instead.

Granted, but they COULD experience joy, couldn't they?

Yes, I guess it's possible.

Okay. What is the difference between the one who does experience joy and the one hundred that do not—if they are all in the same circumstances?

Well, I guess the difference is one of outlook and attitude.

What do you mean by that?

Well, the one sees things differently than the rest.

How might he look at things differently that would not cause him suffering like the others?

Well, let's say that his parents are both enlightened and perfected in Your love already. And let's say that the child understands the value and use of pain. He could be very happy to be able to experience the pain that he does in order to atone for other's sins and to gain merit for his eternal palace in heaven. He may also understand that very soon he is coming to heaven to be with You, as is Your will. He may know that his parents understand this and have no sorrow over his departure; rather they are happy that he will go to his reward before them and they look forward to seeing him in the afterlife. I imagine that even a small child, if not messed up by false beliefs, might be able to see the good in this situation.

And is this the essence of why he may experience joy even in this situation—that he can still see the good in this situation?

Certainly. As long as you can see some good in a situation, you can still enjoy it.

And what is the good that they are seeing?

OH, WOW! I get it now. They are seeing You in this situation. By God, You are right. That IS the essence of joy. I get it now.

And do you think that I want My children to suffer?

No. You may allow us to endure pain, but I don't think that You really want us to suffer. I love Summer and I wish for her to not have to experience any suffering. I certainly would not force her to suffer, although I might force her to endure pain sometimes.

And this is how I am. I am always willing to allow you to see the good in a thing. Why then, Peniel, is there such widespread suffering in the world?

Because You have given us our free will; we are free to refuse to see the good in anything that we choose. We are free to suffer anytime we choose. You don't cause it or wish it upon us; we do it ourselves.

And what do you believe is primarily responsible for the overwhelming amount and intensity of suffering that mankind endures?

The root of all of our problems—false beliefs and ignorance. Such as the belief that there is no good in some thing that we experience. We refuse to even look because we've already made our mind up with this false belief. Hence, we find it impossible to enjoy it.

And is there ever a situation in which you cannot find anything to enjoy?

No, for we can always go outside and look up at the clouds and sky, and down at the birds and grass and nature.

Yes, I have placed such wonderful treasures all around you. If you cannot find anything else that you are willing to enjoy, you can at least experience Me in any aspect of nature and choose to enjoy Me there, if you will. Pitiful is the person who will not enjoy himself among such treasures as I have provided all around him, every day, with generosity and regularity! Do you not know that there are birds and insects and grass and trees and sky and stars outside right now? What would stop you from going right out and enjoying them if you chose to? Only you. There are people and children and animals all around you. All may be enjoyed if you are willing to fully appreciate the beauty and good that is within.

If you were to suddenly come to fully appreciate everything that I have given to you, you should be in a continuous state of rapture and mystical joy. Even if you just allow yourself to fully experience the good that is within your own power and life and ability to choose, joy would be your constant companion. What could ever mar your joy? You may always think, feel, say, and be whatever you choose. You have infinite power of free choice, and this is a beautiful gift more precious than any treasure. Surely you can at least appreciate this in any situation. And in that amount, you can still experience joy, for you will see Me and touch Me within your own power.

Well, thank You for clearing it up.

I desire for all of you to know of Me—and the truths of life. There are few of the important things in life that are not understandable and reasonable

At perfection all things are seen clearly because all things are seen in relation to You. Now I understand this statement a lot better. When things are seen as God sees them, the secrets are all revealed. I love You more than I even know how. Teach me to love You perfectly.

I love you also. Enjoy life fully, Peniel, and teach others to do the same!

CHAPTER 13
Power

Me: I've been doing a lot of writing lately, getting this book entered into the word processor so that I will be able to make copies for others.

God: I know. Don't worry, there's plenty of time. I know that you haven't been recording any of our recent conversations. If I really wanted you to, I would have asked you to record them.

Okay. What do we talk about today?

Power.

Good. This is a very misunderstood subject.

We spoke earlier about the state of the world.

Yes, it's in quite a mess.

And I asked if you thought that it would be in a better state if most people were good, sincere, loving people.

Yes, I remember.

Let's pick up from there.

Okay, shoot.

If most people really chose to be sincere, loving, benevolent people, do you think that your world would be changed for the better?

I don't know. It seems that a very few people make most of the decisions for the majority of the people. If those people who exerted major influence were to become benevolent and sincere and have true personal integrity, that might make a great difference.

And who is it that exerts this great weight of influence?

People who have a lot of power or authority.

And where do they get their power or authority?

From wealth, position, fame, or might.

No, that is a common misperception. There is no power in any of these things. Power is the essence of what we are dealing with. Fame, fortune, might, and authority are only some of the forms that usually contain the essence of power.

Then where does the essence come from?

From Me only! I Myself have given the power to anyone that has power. Any person who has power in any form, gets it from Me.

Yeah, I remember. Pilate said that he had the power either to crucify You or let You go free, and You told him that it was true, but that he wouldn't have it if Your Father hadn't given it to him.

Yes, and it really shook him up. He was very afraid, because, deep down, he knew who I was.

So You mean there is really no power in any of these forms—the power is an essence that You Yourself bestow in whatever form it comes in?

Right. All power comes directly from My Father, through Me.

Give me an example so that I can better understand.

Okay, choose a common form of power.

Money. Surely money is power—and not just the form it takes.

Why do you say that?

Because if you have enough money, you can get many things done. You have a lot of power.

Yes, because money usually contains power. It is one of the common forms I use to contain power. Money of itself has no power and is useless.

I don't get it. Give me an example.

Okay, I give you five million dollars.

Great!

Now, do you have a lot of power?

Yes.

Now you still have the five million in cash, and you are on a deserted island—you will never again be around any other humans. How much extra power do you have because of your cash?

Oh, wow. I get it. It only has power because of other people! With no one else around, it's just paper good for nothing more than burning or wrapping fish in.

Right. There is very little real power in money without other people to give it its power.

And that is the way it is with all power?

Yes. A person would have no power if I did not allow him to have it and did not give it to him.

So everyone that has any form of power got it from You.

Yes, although many of them will refuse to acknowledge this.

But why do You give all that wealth to some people when there are people starving to death all over who could buy food if they just had a little of the rich man's money.

I give them the wealth and give them the desire to give it to those less fortunate than themselves. This way they can gain great merit for willingly sacrificing their excess luxury and doing a very noble thing—loving their fellow man and saving him from certain death.

Why then is there still all of the starvation in the world?

Why indeed. If you divided the wealth of the world equally among the people of the world, how much would each person receive?

A great deal, I'm sure. There is an awful lot of wealth in the world. There's gold and diamonds, natural resources and land, and all kinds of wealth to be divided up.

And if it were divided equally among all of the people?

Each of us would have plenty—and probably quite a bit of luxury also.

And this is My intention. I am no fool. I know how many people I have created on the earth. And I have arranged so that each of My loved children could live in relative ease and financial independence.

Yeah, I see that You have provided well for everyone—yet there are some bungholes hogging most of it!

Yes, and their crime is one of the most terrible crimes of all. I have given each of them the chance to give up most of their surplus wealth and to only keep what is their fair share—the amount that each would receive if all of it were equally divided. Yet few of them have heeded My sweet compulsion. Few of them will receive the great reward prepared for each of them. What a wonderful thing, to willingly give away your surplus wealth to those in poverty.

I see. You have allowed them to receive their wealth so that they could save the very lives of many of Your children. This is a marvelous thing.

Yes, but many of them refuse My gift to them; they choose to remain rich. You remember about the rich man and Me?

Yes. You gave him the same chance, but he loved his wealth too much.

And that is why I said it is so hard for a rich man to get into heaven. How can he justify having so much surplus luxury, knowing full well that My children are starving all around the globe?

And if all of the rich people would give away their surplus wealth to those in need, then everyone would receive his fair share.

Yes, and none would be poor or starving. Figure it out for yourself, reader: if you divided all of the resources and wealth of the earth in all of its various forms among all the people, how much would each one receive?

His fair share—which is quite a lot.

Yes. But having your fair share is not being rich, it is being financially independent. When you have much more than your fair share, and others in the world are starving to death, then you are rich.

So there is nothing wrong with having a lot of money?

Certainly not. Do you think I would have all of the people in the world be poor and look at the wasted goods of the world? I have given you all so much. And as the population increases, so does man's wealth.

How can our wealth increase? Isn't there just so much land, and so much food?

Yes, but there are riches that are beyond just that.

Such as?

The wealth of knowledge that I give mankind through science and technology. Man can now grow more food and have a better life. Innovative tools can save mankind from the necessity of much manual labor. And man continues to discover new resources and better ways of using the resources that he now has. Do you really think that I would send more people into the world if there were not enough resources to properly care for them and give them a comfortable life?

No, I guess not. You do love us. But I thought that poverty was a holy thing.

It can be. Yet I do not intend for everyone to be in holy poverty. Can you imagine a world with all holy poor people with no one to claim or use any of the wonderful resources that I have destined for most of you? They could gather all of the wealth of the world into a big pile and just look at it and wish things were different. Wouldn't that be silly? The important thing is to view money correctly.

Yes, I see Your point. There is a lot of wealth in the world and more resources being found each day. There is plenty for us all. The biggest problem is that very few control most of it—and they are the ones with most of the power; they make the decisions. The decisions they make affect our lives—and they decide to stay rich and leave us poor.

And they shall have to give an accounting for their choices. It is a shame that so few can oppress so many.

But isn't there power other than the power of wealth?

Yes, but wealth is the most common form of power.

So power can be in other forms.

Certainly. It comes to those whom I send it to. Yet I won't force it on you.

And most of us are unwilling to receive the power You want to give us.

Right. The most important power is the power to love. No matter how little money you have, you may be rich in this power anytime you choose to be.

And it is much more important to have that power than to have your fair share of the money in the world.

Right. It is one of the most abused of My gifts.

Yes. The rich worry about how they can keep and justify their money. The independent worry about having too much or too little. The poor worry about having to find next week's food money.

Yes. The vast majority of modern man's time is devoted to thinking about money, sex, and personal appearance. How little time most of them spend considering the essential or important things in life.

I am ashamed for us, yet there are some of us who do think about the important things in life. And I am convinced that the vast majority of people are really good at heart and would only want what is fair and just. They don't want to be rich while their brother starves to death—they would give their fair share. They don't want to hurt another unjustly or seek revenge; they just want to be treated with love and respect. They don't wish to oppress their neighbor or be jealous or prejudiced; they want to live in peace and harmony with all others. They really only want what is good and fair, just and right, and loving and the best for all. And, given the opportunity to accept these things, I believe that most would choose them. The problem is that they are so full of false beliefs, fear, and hate that the choices are not presented to them; or if they are presented to them, they fail to recognize them for what they are. Please have mercy on us all; we are very ignorant and afraid.

I do have mercy on all of you, yet My patience will not last forever. How long will I suffer watching My children being killed and strangled by the arrogance of the few evil men? How long shall I put up with man's noisy lack of faith? How long shall I wait before I say, "ENOUGH!" and come to take the remnant of My true followers away from this hell of man's creation. For the sake of those who will listen and still follow Me, I shall give the world another day, and another, yet I shall not do it forever! Beware; I will come like a thief in the night. Be prepared at all times, Peniel, for you do not know when it will be time.

I am always ready, Jesus. Come when You will.

You are very good, Peniel!

And so are You, my Love.

CHAPTER 14
Perfection

Me: Well, what shall we talk about today?

God: We spoke earlier about perfection; let's recount that conversation.

Okay. You know that I love You.

Yes, and I love you also.

Now, about perfection. Tell Me what you know about it.

I got a little breakout of the letters that I think is kinda cute. It is: **P**erform **E**very **R**equired **F**unction **E**fficiently, **C**orrectly, **T**hrough **I**mitation **O**f **N**one.

That's pretty good. It means to be your true self, all that you are, without any deviation or imitation.

Yeah. Summed up: To be perfect is to be able to perform as you were intended and designed to perform.

Okay, that's a pretty good starting point. Let's go from there.

All right, shoot.

Let's talk about man and his perfection. Is there anything that I created that is imperfect in any way?

No. All that You do is perfect and without fault originally. If something that You have created becomes imperfect, it does so by its own choice. God doesn't make junk!

So you're saying that everything that I create is perfect.

Yes. It couldn't be any other way by the definitions I accept.

What has the power to become imperfect by its own choice?

Only those beings that You have given a free will to.

So if I create a thing and it has no free will, then it must be perfect and remain perfect.

Hmmm. I think that there's a flaw in that reasoning somewhere, because perfect animals would not age or die.

Well, let's assume that this is a result of the curse of the Fall of man, and as such is not the responsibility of nature.

All right. Disregarding the fact that there were many repercussions in nature due to the Fall of man, then yes, everything else is perfect throughout nature and remains this way.

Okay. Remember the story you wrote your daughter called "The Frabbits"?

Yes. It is about some frogs and rabbits that get confused about who they are and what they believe.

Tell Me the main point of the story about them.

Well, the main point of the story was that it is best to be your natural self and not attempt to be what you were not intended to be. There was a rabbit with a bum leg and he had been created that way. He thought that he was imperfect and less than the other rabbits. Because of his bum leg, however, a beautiful fox that had kits one winter and would have starved to death if the rabbit had not been in that place at that time with a bad leg easily caught him. The truth is, in the overall scheme of things, all things that have no choice are perfect and are as they were intended to be. They each fulfill their own mission as God destined it for them.

And what does perfection lie in?

It lies in doing what was intended, and if there is a choice—such as with people—choosing what is best. Basically, it means fulfilling your purpose in being what you should be.

Now, ask Me some questions about perfection.

What should a human being be? What is their purpose?

To be loved and to love perfectly.

And could an animal be imperfect?

No, for they have no choice in the matter. They will fulfill their assigned purpose because they are programmed to and have no choice in it. Only beings with free will may become imperfect—and even they were created perfectly to begin with.

So what do You say that perfection is?

Perfection is being natural.

What about an engine. If it is perfect, what does that mean?

It means that it can perform its designed functions as it is supposed to.

What if it has flaws in it?

It depends; was it designed this way, or did this happen when it was being made?

Let's say that it was designed perfectly, and it got flawed in the creation.

Well, can it still perform its designed purpose correctly?

Yes.

Than it is still perfect. Perfection does not necessarily mean unflawed, it means that it is capable.

Let's say that it can do what it's supposed to do, yet, never does.

Okay, why not?

It is never given the chance. Let's say that it is an engine and it never gets put in a car.

As long as it is capable and willing, it remains perfect. Perfection is not tied to performance, it is only tied to ability and willingness. It is a question of motive, as most everything else is.

And now let's talk about perfection in people. Is there such a thing?

Yes.

Were people created perfect, originally?

Yes. I don't make junk, remember?

When they are brought into the world, are they perfect?

With the definitions for perfection that we have adopted here, yes.

Are we born perfect?

Disregarding the effects of the Fall of man—yes.

Can we remain perfect throughout our life?

Yes. You have that power.

Do most of us remain perfect?

No. Most of you leave your natural state early. You make choices that are not in keeping with what you know is good.

Why?

Two main reasons: fear and false beliefs.

I remember. After we become imperfect, may we reacquire our previous perfect state?

Yes.

What are the two different states called?

The old and new man, the phony and natural self, and so forth.

Is it really possible for an imperfect man to once again become perfect?

Did I not request that you be perfect as your heavenly Father is perfect?

Yes.

Would I ask you to do things that were absolutely impossible for you to accomplish?

No. That would be silly.

Then you can return to your perfection. It is even within your adult power to overcome the problems that were caused by your birth in sin due to the Fall of man.

How can this be done?

You must become as a child again. For as a child you were perfect and natural.

And how is this done?

A man must be born again.

I see. And when you experience this new birth, you are perfect?

Yes; all things are made new. You once again become the true natural you.

And can this be lost also?

Yes. As before, you have the power to throw your true self away; it is your choice.

And to be your natural self, and to make your choices according to love and truth and reason, is this perfection for a person?

Yes, just that. It does not imply that you will never again make any mistakes. Nor does it imply that you will never have a relapse. It merely says that you are now capable of all that you were intended to do, and that you are completely willing and committed to being what I intended for you to be. Notice that no action is needed, only capability and willingness. Motives are the key.

But originally, when a man makes the choice to become perfect, he may have thrown away a lot of the power and capabilities that You intended for him.

Yes. This is usually the case.

And does his accepting of his new birth restore this power to him?

Some, but probably not all.

Okay, I get all this. What else should we say about perfection?

He who loves perfectly is at perfection. At perfection, all things are seen in God and all things are seen with the eyes of God. These eyes see the good within all things, and therefore all things are loved and respected in their proper way. There are some who achieve perfection in this mortal life. All are able to; few are willing to pay the price.

Perfection is the state that I wish for each of My loved children to be in. Until a man achieves perfection, he cannot be loved perfectly. At perfection a man may be loved perfectly, for he is all-good. When a man is loved perfectly and is willing, My Father and I will come and live within him. We shall become one with him. He shall be fulfilled and all that he should be. We shall give him all manner of gifts as is good for him and we shall stay with him as long as he does not drive us away with sin or request us to leave by his own choice.

Man can have all this, if he will only choose what he knows is good. Choose perfection, My children—I love all of you.

And I love You, my darling Jesus. Stay with me forever and love me. Make me all that You wish me to be. I give my all to You.

CHAPTER 15

Our Greatest Barrier To Truth

Me: God.

God: Yes son.

I love You.

I know. I love you too.

Can we talk about something important?

Like what?

Like why we have such trouble with the truth.

What do you mean?

Well, I've noticed many times that when we find the truth, or when the truth comes to us, we either can't or won't accept it. We find it almost impossible to accept the truth! Why is this?

Let Me ask you a few questions to clarify some points for understanding first and then you will see.

Okay.

What is the single largest problem that a person has in coming to be aware of the truth?

Probably the lack of clarity in his life and personality and thinking.

Exactly. As you have learned, clarity is the first barrier to overcome before you will allow yourself to see the truth.

Okay, I got this. What else do You want to ask?

How does a person get clarity on a particular subject?

Simple. He just accepts reason and then questions himself about this particular subject.

Okay, and let's say that he currently has many false beliefs in this area that he is questioning himself about. How will he find out that his current beliefs are not true?

Why, it's simple. Reason will show him.

Are you sure?

Certainly. Reason is always the best guide inward into the land of understanding about beliefs and truth.

Why is that?

Because reason is the light that reveals the truth. Reason is the power that You Yourself have given us to find the truth.

You mean that a person should base his beliefs on what is reasonable?

I would hope that a serious seeker of truth would do just that!

Why is it so important to use reason to find the truth?

Because there are powers that want each of us to be deceived about the truth, and these powers will lead us astray if at all possible.

And what is the best defense against these evil powers?

Reason, a loving and willing heart, a good sense of humor, and a sincere willingness to question one's own dearly held beliefs.

Why be willing to question your own beliefs?

Because only a fool says, "Don't confuse me with the facts or reasonableness; my mind is already made up on this subject!"

Why is this so foolish?

Because once you hold your beliefs so tightly that you are no longer willing to question their validity, then you have cut yourself off from being able to learn the truth—if you are mistaken.

Why is this?

Say you believe that life is not worth enjoying, and this belief is untrue and is causing you a great deal of harm and trouble. If you are not willing to listen to someone else's opinions or stated case of facts or reason, you will not be giving yourself the chance to change your false belief and come to accept the truth. You will not even be willing to listen to reason, even though reason is your only hope to come to the truth and therefore have a better life of love, peace, and joy.

So, if a person is unwilling to see the truth in the first place, what is probably the problem?

Lack of clarity because he refuses to listen to reason.

Are there any subjects where reason should be disregarded when studying or searching for the truth?

No. And there are some subjects where reason alone is not sufficient to fully understand and know the truth about.

Such as?

Such as love. Love is beyond the mere confines of reason. A proper understanding of love cannot be arrived at with reason alone.

Does this mean that when a person studies love to learn the truth about it he should throw reason out the door and ignore anything that reason suggests about love and loving?

Not at all. Reason should still be heeded and listened to, yet a person must understand that on this subject, reason alone will not be enough for a total understanding.

So, should reason always be heeded and sought and listened to when searching for any truth?

Yes, always!

Very good! You have learned well. Indeed, reason should always be your guide, for only reason can lead you fully to the truth!

And what do you think reason is?

Reason is our touchstone to God's truth. It is the mental tool that You have given all of us to use to find the truth.

Very good. Reason should always be sought on a subject because I AM reason. I am reasonable, and except for those things that transcend reason, reason alone is all that is needed to find the truth. If reason is ignored, what truth could a man possibly come to understand?

None. A person without a reason is either retarded or a fool.

And what is a person who has a good reasoning ability and is yet unwilling to use it in some particular area that he wishes to know the truth about?

He's typically human—like we all are at times.

Are you saying that sometimes a person says that he is searching for the truth, yet when reason attempts to reveal the truth to him, he suddenly changes his mind and won't listen to reason anymore?

Yes. This is exactly what I was getting at in the beginning of this conversation. Why do we do this?

Let Me continue the questions and I think that reason itself will pose the answer to you.

Fine, ask away.

As an example let's use a typical person who might come to you after reading this book in the hopes of advancing his perfection.

Okay. Is he serious in his search?

Yes.

Is he committed to the truth?

Well, whether he is or not is hard for you to perceive unless I tell you. It is only important to you in the beginning of instructing a willing learner that you be convinced that he is serious. Let's say that he is serious and comes to you for instructions on how to once again become his true self and achieve the goals that he has established for himself.

All right. We'll assume this. Now what?

Let's say that one day you are teaching him about the nature of God.

Okay.

When you ask him the questions revealing the account that we presented earlier in this book about what I want most is to love you, he finds it difficult to accept this.

Granted. It may be very difficult for even the most sincere seeker of truth to easily accept truths that are foreign to his currently held beliefs. I should know, I had You as my teacher and I had absolutely no doubts about Your integrity and knowledge of the subject matter that You were teaching. Yet I found it difficult at times to accept some of the things that You taught me. And I think that I was about as serious and sincere a seeker of truth as there ever was. Those that learn from me will surely have doubts about my integrity and knowledge of the subject matter in the beginning of my instructions to them. I can certainly understand their caution in areas such as this.

Yes. Yet you realize that if you follow My guidance on how to assist others back to the truth, you will not be the one teaching them.

I know—their own good sound judgment and reasoning will be their teacher. I cannot teach them anything; they can only teach themselves.

This is true. And since you cannot teach them anything, why are you even speaking with them?

As You do for me, I shall do for them. I will be their guide along the path to themselves. I shall assist them to continue along the correct path, and to not turn away when it is tough. I will merely ask them the right questions so that they can find their own reasonable answers. And, when the occasion warrants it, I may put in my own two-cents worth of understanding and knowledge. I may propose alternate answers or solutions that they had not considered before.

So what is your main job with them?

To propose the proper questions, suggest alternate answers, and open locked doors.

A guide?

A guide.

Very good. You understand your part well. You are not there to carry them the entire journey, even though you may at times choose to carry them part way for your love of them and their inability to advance on their own power. Yet, your primary job for them will be as Mine has been for you—asker of the right questions at the right time for their sure advancement in the right direction.

Okay, I got all that. Yet, what about the problem that we all have with not being willing to accept the truth that reason proposes to us at times?

Yes. False beliefs are like a mountain that most people have to tear down in order to return to their true self. And ignoring our own reasoning power is like a wall between that mountain and us. Until you get over the wall, you cannot even begin to work on the mountain.

I understand this. Many times I have experienced this. I'll just get going good with a person and will propose some new concept or question, and bam, just like that, they get real scared and run for the hills. Why is this?

Because of the concept that you are proposing.

Why? All that I do is ask some question. Their own reason is proposing the answer to them. I only ensure that they understand the possible consequences of their choices and decisions in the matter.

Exactly. And this is their great fear at the time.

WHAT?

The new concept.

Why should they be scared by their own reason proposing an answer to some new area of thought that they had not considered before?

They would not be scared if that were the case. And, that is not the case that we are discussing here.

Oh, what is the difference?

Whatever it is that struck a sensitive nerve in them must be something about which they already have dearly held beliefs! If it weren't, they would not be getting in such an uproar about it—they would simply listen to the voice of reason from within themselves, and casually accept what reason suggested to them. The explanation of why it is so difficult is because reason has just proposed some different answer than they have in their current belief system. And, the bigger the fit they throw against their own reason's proposal, the more dearly they must be clinging to their particular false belief being attacked by their reason.

I get it! I always did this with You when You proposed some reasonable idea that went against some belief that I held as sacred to me! I understand why it becomes such a problem for us sometimes—we cling tightly to our old beliefs and ideas.

Even when they are contrary to your own reason?

Exactly! And if this is true, it explains something else.

What's that?

Let me put it into an example. Let's say that I have a dearly held false belief that God cannot sin or lie or do anything wrong.

Okay, for the reader's understanding, let Me ask you a few questions about this example.

Go ahead and ask.

Why do you believe this?

I believe it because my human father believed it dearly and drilled it into me with many examples.

Yet don't you realize that your human father could have been mistaken in this belief?

No; I thought that he was perfect. Remember the parental worshipping when I was a child.

Okay. So you had no reason to doubt that this belief was indeed true. Yet, why is it such a dear and tightly-clung-to idea of yours?

Because when I was young I got into a serious argument about whether God was really good or evil. My opponents had many reasons why they thought that God must be evil. For one, there is so much evil in the world that God at least allows us to endure. And then there are the things like innocent children dying of terrible diseases. They made a very convincing argument about why God must be evil in nature, or that at least he is evil at times.

Okay. And what was the outcome?

Well, the crowd was basically convinced that my opponents had the more convincing case, so many people went away that evening believing that God was evil—at least sometimes.

So?

So, I knew that this was not true. I knew deep down in my heart that God was good. I knew that God would never do anything bad or evil. And this truth became very important to me.

Why?

Because I am secretly afraid that perhaps my opponents were correct. Perhaps God does do evil things at times.

Would you consciously know that you harbor this secret doubt?

No way! I would never allow a fear such as this to surface in my conscious mind. I am afraid to even discuss the subject about God's nature for fear that I may find out that God really is evil. I'm afraid that my own reason will propose the same arguments that I heard my opponents propose that night—and I have no reasonable refutations to these proposals. If it ever comes up, I may learn the truth that I am afraid of learning.

I thought that you were sincere in your wanting to learn all truth.

In this example, the person does not want to learn any truth that goes dead against what he thinks must be right, even though he cannot see the reason why he is right.

So, what does he do when the question about the nature of God comes up?

Runs for the hills.

How?

Lots of ways. I could start a general argument, switch subjects, cloud the issue with a lot of silly or irrelevant questions, evade the issue, and any number of other things. I have learned many neat ways to remain in this dearly held belief before—and I must not discuss it openly and reasonably!

Oh, why not?

Because if I did, I would run the sure risk of having my own reason agree with my opponent. Even then I would still be unwilling to give up my dearly held belief—I know that it must be true, even though I cannot defend it against my own reason.

What would be so wrong with maintaining your chosen beliefs even in the face of opposing reasons? You are a free human—you may choose to believe whatever you wish, right?

No. If my own reason clearly contradicts what I now believe, and I maintain that belief still, then I have become what I detest most in others.

And what is that?

A phony. A hypocrite. A liar. Someone that doesn't practice what he preaches.

So, if you have already subconsciously chosen to maintain this belief no matter what, and you know that reason may suggest to you that you are mistaken if the question comes up, how do you fix it so that you can live with this?

Simple. I play ostrich on the subject. If it comes up, I bury my head in one of my diversionary tactics.

And what are the results of this charade?

I get to maintain both my questioned belief and my outward integrity for being a serious seeker of all truth.

And how do you know that this is the case if someone starts sidestepping some issue?

Because if they are a serious seeker of the truth, they should wish strongly to seek out just such problems as may be lurking within the vault of their beliefs. If there is some belief in there that is indeed unreasonable and untrue, I will want to expose it and discuss it and learn the truth about it for myself—IF—if I am committed to the truth! And that's the key; this person is obviously not really committed to the truth—even if he says that he is. We many times say that we are what we think we should be like, rather than what we subconsciously know that we really are like.

And this is the answer to your question. Let us use an example: A person comes to you and says that he is a sincere seeker of truth. He says that he is truly committed to the truth and finding all of it. Then he starts sidestepping some issue, concept, or idea that you propose. You need to understand that at times a person will say or act in the manner they wish they were, not as the truly are. They do this in an attempt to cover up what they fear they are really like. It is all so silly, for the person accepted false beliefs about how he is, and these are causing him to act in an unnatural way. This act is an attempt to cover up the things in himself he believes are unacceptable to others. The truth is that it is really his false beliefs at the heart of both the mistaken ideas about himself, and the fear that others won't accept him as he truly is.

So the difference is one of commitment to the truth and finding all of it that pertains to our own life and purpose?

Certainly. For why would a person say, "I choose not to discuss or consider what you are proposing," if it were not that he fears that it may prove that he is wrong on that particular subject?

So is it that a person is afraid that he may be proven wrong about this particular idea?

Yes. I'm sure that you remember well your lengthy discussion with Phillips at work some time ago.

Yes, I remember.

What was the problem in having a calm discussion about the nature of God?

No matter what questions that I proposed to him so that his own reason should assist him to see the truth, he sidestepped, countered, and argued until he neither had to concede the point to his own reason or admit that his beliefs were incorrect.

And what were the results of his arguing?

I guess he came off thinking that I was attacking his faith or attempting to prove him wrong.

And here is another of the keys! Sometimes a person believes that you are attempting to prove him wrong—and they would much rather be right than to learn any truth to the contrary! They don't really want to know the truth, or they would willingly listen to new ideas proposed and accept whatever reason truly suggested on the matter. If they couldn't wholeheartedly agree with the point at the time, they would at least be very anxious to further discuss the issue in the hope of shedding new light of reason on the subject.

What did he do after the argument?

He treated me coldly and seemed to remain aloof around me.

What did you get as his message of his treating of you afterwards?

I got this: "Don't talk to me any further on the nature of God—my mind is already made up!"

And how do you feel towards Phillips now?

I feel deep love for him, yet I also feel a little sorry for him. He seems typical of many people that I have talked with who think that they are sincerely seeking God's truth and love, yet I fear for them. Thank You for Your mercy.

Yet I allowed you to discuss this with him just because I wished for him to learn the truth from his own mind's reason. If he refuses to listen to his own reason, then he has pretty well tied My hands from being able to teach him the truth on this subject.

How shall I know when it is truly Your guidance and when it is just my own blabbing?

Peniel, the way to know is to be. So long as you love Me and remain close in My favor, what does it matter whether you or I start your actions? Would you intentionally lead someone astray or harm another unjustly?

Never! I love You and I respect the YOU that is within others—even though they may be unwilling to show that You are in there. I would never willing deceive another or intentionally misguide them.

Then you should not fear anything that you teach. Always remain loving and dedicated to the truth and to loving and serving Me through willingly receiving My gifts of love and service to you, and through your own willingness to teach others. Then you will be the most pleasing to Me. I have created you so that you could guide others seeking truth. I have destined that it be very easy for you to learn these truths and then convey them in a reasonable way to others. This is My will for you; do not deny Me the joy of seeing you do great things merely because you are afraid that you may cause others to be judged more severely because they have not accepted the truth that their reason posed to them as a result of you asking them some questions. I love you and I know that you love Me. Why do you even now remain obstinate in your refusal to casually accept My will for you?

I fear that my teachings may do a great deal of harm to others. If they have some questions asked by me and this causes them to have severe difficulty in their current relationship with You, I am not sure that I want that responsibility.

Then I will tell you how to safeguard others from yourself, if this is your wish.

It is, for now at least.

When a person comes to you and seeks to find truth with your guidance, first be sure to your own satisfaction that he or she is sincere. Then, before you get to those dangerous waters of discussions that you realize are the ones that cause most people the most difficulty, make sure that they understand that you may discuss some things that are very difficult for them to consider. Forewarn them, and if they choose not to venture into these waters for the time being, then respect their wishes; wait until they advance more and then suggest again that you may discuss such matters. If they take the responsibility themselves for seeking all the truths that I wish for you to show them, then this will relieve you of that responsibility.

I am not concerned over being relieved of the responsibility, I simply do not want to do them more harm than good. Even if I do as You suggest here, many people are not fully aware of what is good for them. They may honestly believe in their conscious mind that they are ready for bigger things, yet it may be that they would not receive these difficult matters easily. I do not wish to harm them because I proposed some hard saying that they were not prepared for.

If you feel that this may be the case, then test their sincerity concerning the particular matter. Give them a trial run into the shallow waters of the matter. I had the same dilemma when I came. Just imagine what it was like for Me to be telling the people gathered in the crowd that I was the Bread Of Life that had come down from heaven. The vast majority in the crowds of people listening to Me at that time were simple folk without what you would consider a deep desire to know the truth. A great many of them were merely curious about Me. Yet I proposed to them such a difficult belief to accept that even many of My disciples who had given up everything to follow Me said, "This is a hard saying. Who can take it seriously?"

Yes, I remember. And then You asked them if that shook their faith in You. I guess that I am more afraid of being rejected by those who have come to learn from me than I am of doing them harm with my questions. You wouldn't have done this. You would have simply done what came naturally to You. You always said what You thought You should say, and asked the questions that You thought should be asked at that time. Sometimes I don't do as I feel compelled to because I am afraid that others may reject me due to the uncommonness and strangeness of what I may propose at that time. I could do as You do and always do what I felt compelled to do.

Then, DO SO! I have given you the self-confidence that you need to trust your own feelings. You know what your desires and wishes are, you know of My guidance in your everyday life, you know of My love for you and yours for Me; trust your compulsions. You are very, very good and only your own little remaining fear is between you and the greatness that I wish for you. Overcome your fears and follow Me closely. I shall not let you harm others! I love you and them. You are as yet unaware of much of the good that is done through you. Know that I will use whoever allows Me to use them to do good for the world and My beloved children. I love you all.

Okay, I see. It is my fear of rejection that is more to blame for my unwillingness to teach as I naturally feel compelled to at any given time, rather than my wish to not harm others. I shall remember this. I thank You for revealing yet another of my inconsistencies to complete devotion to You and my assigned mission in life. Will I never totally overcome my own self?

Perhaps not. Yet the important thing is your motives and wishes. You wish that you were totally devoted to Me and doing My will—and this is the more important of the two.

I love You, sweet Father. Thank You for helping me to understand why we sometimes have great difficulty accepting our own reason. I shall remember this the next time someone sidesteps the issues. I shall respect their wish to remain in the dark on it unless I feel compelled otherwise.

Is there anything else that would be proper to put here in this discussion on our greatest barrier to truth?

Yes. Let's talk about a related subject.

Okay, what?

Remember that we talked about the poem "St. Peter at the Gate"?

Yes.

Let's talk about this false righteousness that is demonstrated in that poem. Many people have this feeling of righteousness and supremacy because they think that they have the truth and others are still deceived. Of course, few people who will fit into this category will admit that this might be the case for them. They will say, "Oh, yes. I have known many people who are just as you have described them. Such hypocrites!" And then they will go on their way, just as hypocritical as before. This is such a pitiful state of affairs because a person who is unwilling to consider that they may be incorrect, is doomed to their beliefs.

Was this the reason that You had such problems with the religious leaders when You came?

(Chuckles.) No! I didn't have a problem with them—they had a big problem with Me!

Why were You such a big problem to them?

Many different reasons. One big one was that I threatened them and what they stood for. They were very hypocritical and My being who I am shed great light on their hypocrisy. It was very difficult for them to deal with Me, since that they were supposed to be good and holy men. Oh, they had convinced themselves that they were very righteous; after all, they were the religious leaders of God's chosen people—surely God was on their side. They thought that if I was what some were proposing I was, I would surely come to them and submit to their guidance. Fools! They saw Me doing things that they believed were contrary to God's law—by their interpretation. And they believed that they were the only ones who should interpret what the law meant. They had gone too far in their twisting of My laws given to their ancestors. They were using My laws to heap up large loads for others to bear the burden, while they sat in places of honor. Most of them had become very corrupt and were full of dead men's bones on the inside.

Why else were You such a problem to most of them?

Because I shone the light of reason on the error of their teachings. When I taught, I taught with the authority of reason. When the religious leaders taught, they quoted others rather than proposing valid reasons why what they were teaching was true. Reasonableness and simplicity are the true hallmarks of teaching authority. If what you teach is primarily simple and very reasonable, who could counter it and not seem foolish?

Imagine this scene: A religious leader attacks Me outright in front of many people in the hope of discrediting Me. He wants to show that I disobeyed God's laws. His intention is to make Me appear to be a lawbreaker and a bad person in the eyes of the crowd gathered around Me. He attacks Me by saying, "You do what scripture says not to do.

You perform miracles on the Sabbath." By his interpretation of what was allowed on the Sabbath, I was clearly in the wrong. However, I merely showed the unreasonableness of his interpretation of the meaning of scripture. I said to the crowd very casually and with a smile, "Who among you would not go and get one of your farm animals out if it fell into a ditch on the Sabbath"?

Well, the crowd understood the reasonableness of what I was saying. They also understood that God is not a dictator. Perhaps the limits that the religious leaders had determined about this were unreasonable. They knew clearly that the religious leaders of that day had imposed a great deal of hardship on them through their interpretations of the scriptures, and the crowd viewed Me as a refreshing change from the heavy burden that their leaders had placed upon them. Who wouldn't desire more freedom than less?

None. I see why they had such difficulty with You. Your reasonableness is what gave them some of their problems with You.

Yes. And many of their own people were wishing that I would claim greater authority. I didn't quite fit into their idea of a Messiah. Once again, false beliefs caused the difficulty.

It seems to always be at the root of man's difficulty between You and us.

It is man's greatest barrier. And, coupled with the problem of a person insisting that he is RIGHT, it really creates difficulties.

I have much enjoyed your company this evening. I love you more than you can imagine. Continue to enjoy the wonderful life that I have given you, Peniel. There is so much more destined for you.

I shall, sweet Dad.

CHAPTER 16

The Answer

Me: I have a question that I think everyone eventually asks.

God: Ask whatever you will—I shall answer it for you.

First I must tell You that I love You more than all things.

I know. I love you as only I can love.

Ask your question now.

Oh, God. There are so many problems in the world. There is such trouble on every level of mankind's existence...

WHAT IS THE ANSWER TO OUR PROBLEMS?

I am glad you asked that. I know that many of My children eventually get around to considering this vexing question. The answer, My children, is quite simple and is common knowledge. You put it in songs and write poems about it and whisper of it in the dark—and still you do not get it! **I AM THE ANSWER!** I AM LOVE, and in your terms—Love is the answer.

Does that mean that simple love is the solution to all of the trouble and problems of mankind, the world, and each individual person in his or her daily life?

Absolutely! Mere Love, Pure Love, ME; that is always the answer and solution.

How is this?

Let Me demonstrate to you that the awesome power of pure Love is the only possible solution to any problem dealing with man on any level. Give Me a problem and I shall show how the love of man can solve it.

There is starvation in many places in the world today. This day, untold numbers of people will die of hunger.

I have provided ample food for all of you, and shall always do so. If those who had surplus would Love those in need and give them the extra food and resources that they have, hunger would end. Love is the answer. So long as one man hates another and withholds the extra food that he has from him, there will be starvation in your world.

In each new problem, the same things I have stated here shall apply, so I shall simply state the obvious solution. You may see the other ways that these principles apply—if you will open your eyes.

Peniel, state as many different problems as you think people may pose as unsolvable and I shall provide the solution in general terms. Understand that these solutions may all be done this very day—if you, My children, choose to do so. If you cannot do all of it yourself, then at least do what you can! Do not refuse to do the good that you can just because you cannot do all good.

I leave these answers in your capable hands, reader. You can assist Me to bring peace and harmony to yourself, your family, your neighbors, and—in part—to the world itself...

IF YOU WILL ONLY FOLLOW THE THINGS SET DOWN HERE!

Ask all of the perplexing troubles and problems that you can think up, Peniel. Perhaps through the principle of Love demonstrated here, some shall be enlightened to the answers and shall get off their seats and change their lives and the lives of those whom they touch. Ask away.

Okay. I will assume that I am a typical unenlightened reader of this for the sake of the questions. I myself understand many of these questions and the solutions, yet there are many who will read this that would benefit from the questions posed, so answer me as if I were one of those persons.

I shall. Ask all of your questions now.

First: What is the meaning of life?

Love is the answer. I am the very life you speak of. I am love. What gives your human life meaning is when I am recognized in it and shown through your life. IF you would Love purely, as I love you, then your life would have meaning to you and you would understand. Until you are living life as it was intended, it will be very difficult for you to experience the peace of mind that comes from understanding that the meaning of life is—LOVE. What is the meaning of life? Love is life's meaning. Love is the answer.

Why do I wake up at three in the morning sometimes, and think to myself, *Is this all that there is to life? Isn't there more to it? Shouldn't I be doing something important? I feel that my life is a waste and serves no valid purpose. Why am I here? What am I supposed to do?*

Love is the answer. You ask first, "Is this all there is to life"? I answer you, No! There is so much more to life than what you are now allowing yourself to experience of it. There is more—and the more is Pure Love.

Then you say, "Shouldn't I be doing something important"? And I answer you, Yes. You should Love. And what should you love? Love all that is good and noble. Love Me, for I AM. Love Me by keeping My commandment to you. And this is My commandment to you: Love Me through Loving yourself and Loving your neighbor as yourself. Each of you: Love one another as I have Loved you. Do this and you shall be filled with peace, joy, and fulfillment. And you shall change everyone around you and do much for the world.

All of the world's greatest people have been those who were willing to love more. This is why they became great. Others recognize that greatness is the willingness and ability to love more intensely and purely—nothing more. Love all good and I shall fill your cup with all manner of good things. Love is the answer to your hidden feelings of a wasted life. You can be greater than any other person who has gone before you.

Why do you feel this emptiness and void in your life at times? Because you have not yet accepted full responsibility to be all that I have destined you to be—a perfect lover. Learn to love perfectly and your life shall be full of all that you wish. Love is the answer.

It seems to me that many times others do not like me. How can others better like me?

Love is the answer. If others really do not like you, then there is a reason. If they like anyone at all, then they could like you. If you had the attributes and characteristics that they liked in a person, they would like you.

And here is what people like most in another: The willingness to share in joy. The willingness to acknowledge the good that they contain. The willingness to accept them just as they are and not demand or expect them to change. The willingness to appreciate them and the good that is in them. The willingness to say that they are appreciated. The willingness to admire the outstanding parts that they do have.

Each person has some special talents, abilities, or characteristics that God has given to none but them—they should be admired for their greatness within them.

And lastly, the willingness to adore them if they become all good.

These things sum up what a true friend is to a person. There are many things that you could name that are the qualities that you wish in a friend—and they are all here. This is love.

Love has five stages of purity as man normally shows it. Each higher stage is more pure than the others. The stages are: acknowledge, accept, appreciate, admire, and adore. There is much about them contained in some of Peniel's other books and in his seminars, and this is all that need be touched upon about them for now.

How can you get others to like you better? Learn to love them better. Love is the answer.

I have heard that some babies die of diseases early in life. What is the answer to this problem?

Love is the answer. The "problem" that you see is a blessing in disguise. To whom is the death of a small child a problem? Not to Me. I love all of My children and desire some of them to come to Me early in their mortal lives. Why is this perceived as a problem by so many? Do you not know that the child who dies and comes to be with Me is in a far better place? Do you not realize that they are much happier here than they would be if they remained in the world of sorrow and suffering that you all have made it? Perhaps if I had allowed them to live until the age of reasoning, they would have committed some grievous sin and never repented—thusly condemning themselves to eternal separation from Me and the pleasures of heaven.

Do you know the future or can you fathom all that is in the mind of God? If you could see things with the eyes of pure love, you would see that much of what you pose to yourself as terrible things or problems is really the best thing. Know this: if it happens and there is nothing that any person could have possibly done about it, then I Myself determined it. If I Myself determined it then it is the best possible thing for all concerned.

I am good and I know all things. If you had Pure Love with which to see clearly My workings in such matters, you would not see them as problems. The only problems that you really have are the problems that you create for yourself or that I allow you to endure because they are in your ultimate best interest.

Some children do die young, but it is not a bad thing! It is a good thing. The real problem is that you view it as a problem. And how can this problem of your false perceptions be overcome? Love is the answer. If you would follow My instructions and become your natural self, you would not see good as a problem. Learn to be what you were intended to be by learning of Me—Love—and you shall not be deceived. Love is the answer.

Sometimes I worry a lot about whether we will be able to pay all of our bills and have enough money left to buy the proper food that we need.

Who is the cause of your financial problems? You yourself are the cause of your financial difficulties. Do you have too many bills? You were the one that signed them and bought the things that you really did not need. Why? Do you not make enough money at the job you perform to live at the type of life you desire to live at? Who has accepted the job at that salary? You. Do you seem to have bad financial luck and every investment that you make turns sour on you? Who chose those bad risk type investments? You did.

Do you not know that I love you and am willing to take good care of you? Look at the birds. They don't work—they don't have jobs. Yet I take good care of all of them! And you are My beloved child; you are worth far more than any bird! Why is it then that I am not taking good care of you? Because you are not allowing Me to! I will not force My gifts on you. I love you too much to become your dictator. Why will you not accept these wonderful gifts that I have prepared for you? This is the real problem.

There is plenty of wealth and resources to go around. Your fair share is a great fortune indeed. Why have you not accepted it? It is just waiting for you to take the steps necessary to acquire it. Why do you not set out to make your fortune—if that be your wish for now? Because you do not believe in Me or in yourself! This is the reason.

This, then, is the real problem: You do not have enough confidence and trust in yourself, or Me, to take the necessary chances and steps to achieve the financial status that is best for you. Do you not know that there are thousands just like you who finally get up the courage to venture out into the world and make their fortunes? They are no better or smarter than you. But they have one quality that you still lack: faith in themselves and Me. If you had the faith in yourself that you could indeed achieve the goals and dreams that you have, then you would begin. You have not yet begun? Why is this? The problem is that you do not love yourself enough to trust yourself. You say to yourself, "Perhaps I shall fail and look foolish. Perhaps I shall wind up worse than I am now. I had better not attempt it. It's too dangerous for someone like Me."

If you were really intended to have a certain amount of wealth that I have destined for you, and you trusted yourself and Me enough to do everything in your power to achieve it, do you really think that I would let you down? No. I love you. I want you to do well. Yet I can do nothing until you trust in both of us. If I am willing to take such good care of even grass and insects, would I not be willing to take great care of you and do all that is best for you? Why have I not done so? You have not yet allowed Me to.

Learn to love yourself and Me, and then you will trust yourself and Me. And when you have the trust, the self-confidence that I have destined for you shall return to you. Then you will be able to achieve all of the goals that I have established for you. And they are far greater than the dreams that you have yourself. Nothing can stop you from achieving all this—nothing except YOU. Love yourself and then you can accept all this. Love is the answer.

I don't seem to be as happy as I would like to be. How can I be happier?

Love is the answer. What is it that brings a man happiness? What is the secret to joy in life? How can you be filled with peaceful joy and pleasure? The answer is simple. Love is the answer. Do you not remember your childhood? Do you not realize that you took great pleasure in just being alive? Do you remember smelling a flower for the first time, or seeing Santa, or going to a birthday party, or going fishing with your dad, or seeing your mom smile because you had done something really good? Do you not remember that you took such great pleasure in the simplest things? Do you not remember when you laid on your back looking up at the clouds, picturing them as animals? Do you not remember dreaming of being a fireman or detective or doctor or whatever? Do you not remember watching your favorite comedy? Do you not remember your first girlfriend, or your first kiss? Do you not remember the joy of touching a girl? Do you not remember the fulfillment of being one of the guys in your group? Do you not remember playing games and running and jumping and such things? Do you not remember all of the simple joy and happiness that filled your life—long, long ago?

What has happened to all of these simple joys? Why do you no longer enjoy all of it? It is still just as enjoyable! There are still clouds to see, and dreams to dream, and friends to enjoy, and girls to touch, and family to be with, and a million simple joys surrounding you at every turn. Look around you! Do you not see the flowers? Do you not know that if you were to sit down in the grass in your yard and look carefully at a small part of the ground that you would discover hundreds of marvels of life, all of which could be greatly enjoyed?

Do you stop and look at an anthill for five or ten minutes to see their busyness? Do you wonder about the stars and how many there are? Do you see the children in the park playing on the slide? Do you hear the laughter of your own children? Do you hear the words "I love you" coming from those around you? Do you appreciate the sacrifice that others are now making for you? Do you understand that there are many who think that you are a great person? Do you realize that many people care about you and value you as a person?

Life is live! Join in! Here is where it is, now is when it is, YOU are what IT is! Come back to the appreciation of all of life's wonders and simple pleasures. Allow yourself to fully enjoy all that I have given to you. Did you hear that bird today? As you were walking along, feeling like your normal unhappy self, I sent a wonderful bird near you. The bird sang his best—just for you. I sent him to cheer you up. But, as with most all of the treasures that I have bestowed upon you with generosity and regularity, you ignored and did not appreciate it. I sent the bird for you alone! There was no one else around to hear or enjoy his beautiful song. You alone could have enjoyed that moment in that place.

Why do you refuse to enjoy yourself, life, nature, and others? I have given you so much! You are so fortunate, and yet you do not appreciate it. And the problem is not that there is nothing to enjoy, the real problem is that you refuse to enjoy anything. And the little that you will allow yourself to enjoy, you do not allow yourself to fully enjoy! You have become your own worst enemy. You will not allow yourself any pleasure. I send you many things that you could take great joy in; but I shall not force you to enjoy them.

Why do you not allow yourself to enjoy life's treasures? You do not purely love yourself. There are people in much the same situation as you are and they enjoy themselves tremendously. They laugh and smile, and they feel great when they wake up. They just can't wait to go out into the world on another day and see what treasures I have prepared for them on that new and glorious day. They fear almost nothing and they enjoy almost everything. The difference between them and you is that they Love with a pure heart. They love themselves, Me, and their neighbor. Since they have so much love and their love is so pure, they allow themselves to fully enjoy everything. They have few problems and they have marvelous personalities and outlooks on life. The psychologist Abraham Maslow calls these people, Self-actualized people. This means people who realize their full potential.

This is the key—they have allowed themselves to become more of what they could be than you have now allowed yourself to be. The closer you are to being your true self, the greater is your joy and excitement in life. Let Me show you all of the wonders that I have placed here for your enjoyment! Let Me love you! Come back into My waiting and loving arms. Let Me share My joy with you. Open your eyes and see! Become your true self again.

The problem is that you do not fully enjoy yourself, life, and nature because you are not what you should be. The key element that you lack is pure and intense love. Love is the answer.

There is a great concern among most of the people of the world that we might have a nuclear war and that it would be worse than anything the world has ever seen. How can this terrible war be prevented?

There are some things that are destined and foretold, but it is within man's power to change the very course of history. What is to stop man from bringing peace on earth—if all men choose it and work towards it? If all men were willing to live in trust of each other then there would not be this massive threat that you have created towards each other. Why is man so afraid of his fellow man? Why do you start wars and fight your neighbor? Because you are insecure in your own personality. If you felt secure in your own mind, you would not feel this strong compulsion to defend yourself against everything outside of you. When the time came, I did not defend Myself.

I say to you, resist not evil. Rather, be your true self and evil shall not overcome you. I shall turn the evil others do to you to good and you shall profit from it. Be your natural self and love as you should, and you shall not have these fears—you will find My favor. If you had My favor, and if your relationship with Me were good and sound, would I allow you to endure some hardship that was not in your best interest? Why do you concern yourself over such matters?

There is evil in the world and there shall continue to be evil for a time. You should rather concern yourself with doing what you were sent here to do. Love Me and follow My guidance for you. This is what is most important for you right now. Do this, and everything else will fall into its proper place for you.

I am very powerful and if I am for you, who can stand against you and win? If all men would do this then there would be peace in the world. If all men trusted their fellow man, then there would be no fear of war. Peniel's book *Utopia*, about the supposedly perfect society of man, deals with all of this in detail. This is enough spoken of it here.

The problem is that man fears his brother because he is not secure in his own mind. If he were his true self, if he loved purely, he would have no fears such as this. Love is the answer.

This should be enough for them to get the idea, Peniel. Let us stop the questioning here. For no matter what the problem or difficulty a person may pose, **LOVE IS THE ANSWER!**

Be patient with all of us, Father, for we are so ignorant and so stubborn.

You may be a great help to Me if you shall remain in My love. Continue to follow in My footsteps.

CHAPTER 17
Eliminating Pain And Suffering

God: Okay. Start the seminar now. I will take the part of the audience.

Me: Good evening, my friends. I am Peniel. I am very pleased that you have come this evening. I sincerely hope that we all obtain a great deal of useful wisdom that shall help us tremendously in our daily lives. I offer this workshop free to all of you because I love all of you. This workshop is dedicated to the greater glory of God. It is entitled "Eliminating Pain And Suffering." Are there any questions before I start?

Yes, I have a question.

I just knew You would!

I'm not real clear on the meanings of the words pain and suffering. I know that you usually have very specialized meanings for some words. To clarify exactly what they mean, please give us your intended meaning.

I'm glad that You asked. According to Webster's, pain is taken from the Greek word poine, which meant payment. Webster's primary definition is Punishment. Other definitions are: Usually localized physical suffering associated with bodily disorder (as with a disease or an injury), and The basic bodily sensation induced by a noxious stimulus, received by naked nerve endings, characterized by physical discomfort and typically leading to evasive action.

Webster's says that suffering comes from the Latin root sufferre, which means to bear. Webster's primary definition is: To submit to or be forced to endure. Another definition is: To endure the mental state of distress. Is everyone with me so far?

Yes.

For my own purposes, I make this major distinction between the two: <u>pain</u> deals with physical things, and <u>suffering</u> deals with emotional things. Heat, if it is too intense, will cause <u>pain</u>. The burn scars may make you ashamed and you will <u>suffer</u> embarrassment. Do you all get the difference that I mean between the two?

Yes.

I have some very specialized meanings for these two words that are covered in a workshop on understanding. I shall not recover all of that information here. It is enough that we all recognize that we know what pain and suffering is in our own personal lives, for we have each experienced it in no uncertain terms. It doesn't matter what exact definitions we use in this workshop to define these two terrible things, let's just sum them up and call it feeling bad. Whatever we consider against our choices of what we should like to feel, that's part of it. It's all bad.

How did it all get started?

As God created Adam and Eve, they experienced no pain or suffering. God did not deem it good for man, as he is supposed to be, to endure pain or suffering. It is not within OUR natural order of things.

Isn't there some evil that cannot be stopped?

Perhaps there is some pain and suffering that God has determined that you WILL have to endure, when the time for it comes; perhaps it is his will. It is not within our ability to modify the will of God or prevent or alter this particular pain or suffering. Therefore, it is best—even though we may not understand this. Since this pain and suffering—which we shall call <u>inevitable</u> by the will of God—is good for us and should not be changed, we shall not discuss it here.

Okay. But where does most of our pain come from?

WE cause, allow, create, invent, make, or set up about ninety percent of all of the pain and suffering that we endure, unless we are already perfected in our love of God and fellow man.

What about the rest?

The other ten percent you do not cause. I will call all influences and powers, such as Satan and demons, evil. Of that ten percent, nine-point-nine percent is caused by evil. That leaves only about one tenth of one percent that is actually the inevitable will of God that you must endure.

Why does God decide that we will endure even a little pain?

Let us first speak of the vast majority of your pain and suffering—that ninety percent that you yourself are instigating. WHY? Why would a sane person cause himself such anguish? Think! You are causing—or at least allowing—the vast majority of your own current pain and suffering. And, subconsciously, you are aware of this fact. What possible reason would you or your subconscious have for setting you up for such trouble? Consider this question for a moment before we continue. Ponder this and see if you can come up with a reasonable answer—if what I say is true.

We don't know. It seems crazy, yet we're pretty sure that we do bring much of it upon ourselves, just as you have said.

Let us explore together the reasons through some typical examples. We'll look at others and perhaps some light shall shine through onto our own actions and motives.

Okay, give us an example.

Here's the first situation: Jeff goes out drinking with several of his buddies. They get a little drunk, and then Jeff pulls a real cute stunt. In this crowded bar, Jeff finds the biggest, ugliest, meanest looking monster of a man that he can and proceeds to pour a beer all over his head, for no apparent reason.

That seemed like a real dumb thing to do.

Now, I am sure that you understand that Jeff is in the process of causing himself quite a bit of suffering. He was a little drunk, but he's not stupid. I ask you: Why did he do this?

I don't know. It seems like there wasn't any reason to do it.

This much I have surely learned about human behavior and motivation: all actions of a human being that are voluntary are done with a reason, and each time they are believed to be in the individual's best interests at the time. And ninety-nine percent of a person's actions are done for the same reason: the satisfaction of a particular need. What possible need or needs do you think Jeff is going satisfy through his choice of this action?

Probably the need to get killed!

Let me give you a short list of some of the basic psychological needs: Acknowledgment, Attention, Acceptance, Appreciation, Admiration, Forgiveness, and Compassion. Do you see how Jeff is setting up to get some of these needs fulfilled through this action of his? There should be no doubt that Jeff is going to get a lot of attention from this act. First of all, he's got the monster's attention. He's also got the attention of his buddies and the attention of everyone in the whole bar. As a matter of a fact, it got real quiet for a minute as everyone just looked at Jeff. He was the star of the moment and was in the spotlight.

As you can imagine, the outcome of Jeff's actions was going to be a busted face. Naturally—he didn't pick out some wimpy little guy that he might have a chance at beating in a fair fight. He picked out a Mac Truck to fight. He obviously wanted this guy to beat him up! So, Jeff gets what he wants—a rearranged face; it's all cut and bruised, and will be this way for several weeks. Oh joy; just think of how much attention Jeff will get from everyone that he sees. They'll ask him all about it and he can recount the story for hours on end. Lots of attention. And then he'll get plenty of compassion. "Oh, you poor thing—does it hurt"? But the key to his particular choice of actions is forgiveness. This is the outstanding need that underlies his choice of actions here.

We don't see how that fits in with what he did.

You see, his buddies HAD to come to his rescue and get hit a few times in the ensuing brawl. And now, for weeks, Jeff can go to one of his buddies and say, "Eric, man, I'm really sorry for what I did. It was really stupid, man, and I'm sorry that you got hurt defending me." And then, if he wants to, he can add, "And I'm sorry that I'm such a drunk. I'm sorry that I'm a pain in the butt. I'm sorry that I embarrassed you. I'm sorry..." He can be sorry about a lot of things. And if he doesn't get enough forgiveness from Eric, he's got four other guys that were there also that he can go apologize to. He can milk this for weeks, and if it gets old, he can do something else really harmful and stupid and start all over.

You know, I've known people who did just that kind of crazy stuff every once in a while. And he'd go around apologizing over and over until he drove everyone crazy.

Do you see just how well planned this little game was. Ingenious! And this is how our subconscious mind works. Of course you couldn't ever convince Jeff that this was why he did it. He says that he was drunk and just did it. But we know better. We wouldn't confront Jeff with this truth, for that would expose his game; and he couldn't have that.

Is that all there is to why he did it?

It goes much further and deeper than this, for our subconscious mind is a master of games; yet this should be enough explanation to see a lot of what's really going on. This much is for certain: Jeff's suffering was his own doing in this instance. He caused it; he honestly thought that it was best for him at the time and that he needed it! And this is our big mistake.

What mistake?

We really don't need this suffering. We don't really need any of this pain that we are currently enduring. If we are causing it because we think that it is good for us—and we are mistaken and won't even acknowledge this—we're hurting ourselves needlessly. We need none of this world's pain, suffering, disease, humiliation, or sickness. We can get our needs met perfectly well through other avenues and means. And the other ways do not cause any others or us any undue harm, pain, or suffering. Why cause suffering if it is not good or needed?

I don't know. Why are we like this?

The problem lies in our false beliefs. We mistakenly believe that this is the best and easiest way to get our needs met. We have learned most of this through example.

Like how?

I know a person who I believe is a hypochondriac. I feel great pity for her and her family, not so much because she endures a lot of suffering, but because she needlessly causes herself such pain and suffering. And as you can imagine, her children have similar problems as well. They learned through her example that this is the way to get attention and to get much of what they want. The tragedy is that there is so much real pain and suffering that they are causing to themselves and others; and through their examples they are making others more susceptible to this game. I pray for her and all like her that have adopted damaging games such as these because they knew no other way to receive the love that they desperately need. Have mercy on all of them, Lord; they know not what they are doing.

Can these things be learned in other ways?

Yes. Let me give you another example of how we might learn these bad habits. Dad likes to come home most every day and tell what a rotten day he has had to get mom to say, "Ah, you poor dear." He receives the attention and compassion he needs.

And mom likes to burn the toast in the morning so dad will complain about it. She thinks, *At least this way he knows that I exist in the morning.* And she can say, "Oh, I'm so sorry. I've burned the toast again, dear."

Sounds like My house.

Dad forgives her, just as he does every morning that they carry out this rehearsed ritual. Dad thinks that she must be dingy because she can't make toast without burning it. He doesn't understand that she MUST burn the toast, or else he will just ignore her and she won't get her morning forgiveness from him that she finds so important. If only dad could learn to give mom forgiveness in other ways and pay a little attention to her in the morning, mom wouldn't have to burn his toast. Doesn't he ever notice that she doesn't burn anyone else's toast? No— he's too busy with the morning paper. And she doesn't even understand why she burns his toast.

WHY ARE WE ALL SO BLIND? These little games are saying, "HEY, I'm a person too! Give me a little of what I need!" But, no, we will not see. We refuse to admit our own deception; we will keep playing these same games and causing our own suffering—UNTIL...?

All that we really have to do is to watch our own lives carefully and examine these little games and inconsistencies in our actions. Then we will be able to see what is being done and asked through our actions, if we wish to.

What is the key ingredient to this difficulty?

Adam and Eve, before the Fall, had the same basic needs as we do now, except the need for forgiveness. And this is the key to why we do many things that we were not intended to do. It appears to me, as I have watched many people closely for several years, that most of us have this obsession with setting up reasons so that we can ask and get forgiveness from another. We say, "I'm sorry," through our words and actions most of the time. WHY? Well, we know that if we act like we are really sorry and then ask for forgiveness, the other person HAS to forgive us. It's one of the rules! To do otherwise is to break the rules; and if you break the rules everyone will chastise you. You MUST forgive someone if he sincerely asks you for your forgiveness—at least that's what the rules say.

So, how do we stop playing this game when we finally decide to?

It's easy, but not simple. You must find out why you play. And I will tell you now—you play so that you can WIN. And in this game, to win means to get your need met, whether it is the need for attention or forgiveness or whatever. You must find a way to still win without PLAYING the old harmful game. If it is the need for attention and forgiveness, you don't have to get your face busted and your friends' faces busted in the process. You can find alternative ways to get your needs met. We are all human, until our own individual perfection, so we shall continue to have these same needs. We should find non-hurting ways to get what we need.

This will improve our lives and lower drastically the amount of pain and suffering that we currently are enduring. When we can get most all of our needs met without having to resort to causing pain or suffering, then we will eradicate most of that ninety percent of pain and suffering that we are now enduring.

Can this really be done?

There are many people around, just like you, that experience much less pain and suffering than you currently do. Why do you think this is? Are they very lucky, or does God love them more than you? No, for this is not reasonable. The major differences between you and those like you who endure very little pain and suffering are in attitude and beliefs, but MAINLY in the ways that they have learned to get their needs met. I shall not discuss here the details of the way a person would go about overcoming these problems, for that is the subject of one of the seminars that I teach. It cannot be amply or correctly illustrated in the time that we have here. If you are interested in this seminar, contact me later.

Tell us at least something about how to overcome the evil we do to ourselves.

I will discuss what is the general outline for overcoming these harmful habits and games. They are:

Acknowledge that they exist.

Identify the specific games you're playing that are causing you trouble, pain, and suffering.

Examine the game or habit to see what the prize of that game is.

Identify the benefits and costs of the game.

Decide whether you wish to stop, modify, or continue this game.

Discuss your findings openly with an appropriate counselor.

Establish some goals (like finding alternate ways to win without the same costs).

Set up a workable plan to accomplish your established goals.

Take ACTION, remain consistent, and persevere.

Review your goals, and establish new ones when these are met.

These are the general guidelines and steps for modifying the games that are causing this big chunk of your current suffering.

How do we win the game we play and get the prize?

I'm sure that you realize that there are many possible different ways to win and many different prizes to get. An example is the prize of attention. Rather than being a pain in someone's side and getting your attention this way, you could give them a sincere compliment. This would not only get you the prize of the attention that you wish, it would also make the other person feel better. I'm not saying to be phony or make something up, just open your eyes and look for the good in another—you will find plenty! All people are really good at heart and there is much about each to be complimented sincerely. Why pick on another and point out their faults if they won't learn from your reproach or change and become better? Instead, compliment them on some good aspect that you see in them. In addition to receiving the attention that you are seeking, you will spread love and joy all around. Great are the benefits of not causing pain and suffering through your games, but rather, sincerely spreading love and joy through being your natural self. Try it—you'll like it.

I just can't picture Myself doing that.

Well, how about doing something nice and unexpected for a friend? They'll say to you, "Man, that was great of you. Thanks!" and they will really mean it. You will receive something greater than mere attention—you'll receive some fulfillment. Do it and see!

Is this going to take care of most of our self-inflicted wounds?

Most, but there is a problem with this system. It doesn't work well with the need for forgiveness. That's because you have created this monster of a need for forgiveness. One of the biggest reasons we need all this forgiveness is because the real us—hiding deep within the closet of our subconscious—knows full well all of the evil, pain, and suffering that we are causing ourselves and others. We do all this harm in an attempt to get our needs met. We do it this harmful way because that is the way we were taught to achieve our goals, and we don't know any other way to get what we need.

We have seen some of the harm that we have done in the past through our games, and we hated ourselves for the evil that we had caused. So, to avoid having to constantly deal consciously with the guilt, we started suppressing the truth to ourselves. We refused to admit that we were hurting others, or we justified what we did. Regardless, the truth is seen deep down. We know the hundreds that we have hurt and the pain and suffering we have caused just to get what we wanted and needed. We didn't want to hurt anyone, but we didn't know any other way to get our needs met—and we had to get these needs met!

Shouldn't we go over in our own minds the bad things that we have done in the past?

The milk that is spilt is sour. And yet, there it stands. The question is: now that we are aware of it, will we do something about it? I guess the majority say no, but there are a few special ones who are ready to overcome their suffering and get back to joy in life. Since you have come to this workshop tonight, instead of going bowling, you're probably those people. Have you noticed that there are some people who don't seem to have this overwhelming need to hurt others so that they can then be forgiven? And some of these special people don't play most of these silly grown-up games; some of them have lives with little pain and suffering—their lives are instead filled with joy and aliveness! What a treasure, for what is important beyond doing what you should do and then fully enjoying yourself and your life? To really like yourself, and enjoy yourself and your life, this is a very high goal indeed. Yet many around you have just these things.

What is their secret?

I will tell you. They have little guilt, and they cause themselves and others little if any pain or suffering. They do not create reasons why they should hate themselves and dislike their life and others. They have the natural results of loving themselves, and enjoying themselves, their lives, and others. Their lives are full of joy and peace! I know, for this is the way my life has been for years—ever since I overcame my games and guilt, and my need for forgiveness and hurting others.

Does this type of life appeal to you? I hope that it does. If it does, know that it is just the natural type of life that you should be having anyway. Life is marvelous, if you don't have any reasons or excuses to not enjoy it. If you would like to enjoy life more than you currently do, come to whatever programs you think will be good for you. I have written and often hold a series of "Improvement Training Seminars" free of charge. Attend some of them—they'll change your life and allow you to experience that joy and aliveness that a lot of us seem to have lost since childhood. I shall assist you if you are sincere. My price is very reasonable—I charge nothing! All that is required is your time and sincerity. If you doubt that life can be this way, come and meet me and know me as I am for a while. You will see that my life is full of joy and love, and wonder and aliveness. It is only natural this way; I wish it for you also, if that be your will.

How does a person get rid of this suffering in his life?

You see, when you stop abusing other people to get your needs fulfilled, and instead get your needs met through the natural course of loving others and spreading joy, then you will not be obsessed with this need for forgiveness all the time. You will regain your self-confidence, aliveness, and joy in life and the ability and willingness to love properly and purely. So, here in a nutshell is the first rule to overcoming most of the current pain and suffering that you are enduring in your life:

RULE #1: STOP HURTING OTHERS TO GET WHAT YOU WANT.

Rather, get what you want through loving others and spreading joy. Then you will not have this monster of a need for forgiveness that now causes many of your harmful actions.

Will doing this cause much of a change in My life?

When you learn how to and sincerely follow this rule, your life will change drastically, and most of your current pain and suffering will be gone. In place of it will flow joy and peace and satisfaction. Now, let's assume that your life is already this way, and that you have been doing this for some time. Perhaps you have successfully completed my seminar or you have achieved this naturally in your own life, or maybe you never had this bad situation initially. Now I will tell you how to eliminate the vast majority of the remaining pain and suffering in your life. If it is still not absolutely necessary and is doing no good, we should still attempt to eliminate what we can of it. There will be some, perhaps, that is inevitable for us, as I have said. If this is so, we shall endure that amount and do the most good that is possible with it. The remaining ten percent is far less than what most endure, but our goal here is to eliminate all of our pain and suffering possible, and then do the most good and derive the greatest benefit from all that remains. The second rule will accomplish both of these points.

What is it?

Before I give the rule to you, let us examine the ten percent of pain and suffering that remains in your life. You are not causing it, yet it is there. If this is true, it is either inevitable, or it is not. We will only speak here of that which is not inevitable. It is being sent to you or forced upon you by evil forces.

What do you mean, evil forces?

Satan is the bringer of sorrow. He dearly loves to see man suffer, so long as it serves his needs. Satan has free will also, and has a choice in whether or not he will cause you pain and suffering much of the time. For the person who is not causing himself pain and suffering, Satan and his band are causing most of what he is experiencing.

So what can we do about this?

We can get Satan to stop causing us most of the pain and suffering that he is currently sending us, if he has a choice in the matter.

How?

The answer lies in understanding Satan's motives and reasons for sending us this pain and suffering. If it is like a game and he is currently winning through causing us the pain and suffering, all we have to do is find a way to beat him at his own game—turn the tables on him. If there are rules to this game, let us find out what they are and use them to our best advantage to achieve our own goals.

The first thing to grasp and understand is that God allows Satan free reign sometimes to do with us as he will. If you are not familiar with the book of Job in the Bible, I strongly suggest that you carefully study it soon. It holds many important items we must understand for the proper application of these principles. It tells why Satan is sometimes allowed such control and power over our lives—why God allows him to do to us as he chooses. It also demonstrates Satan's motives and wishes. It tells what the prize of this game is and what many of the rules are.

Why does Satan do what he does?

The main reason why Satan chooses to make us suffer or endure pain is twofold: One, he hates and is very jealous of a just and good person, and two, he hopes that the pain and suffering will turn us against God. His main motivation is to separate man from God. This is the prize he is shooting for. There are certain risks that he takes in playing, but since few people that he plays with are even remotely aware of the rules, he will take the risks.

What risks?

The main risk he takes involves knowing that pain and suffering can be a great weapon and tool in the hands of an enlightened individual. It can be used to advance you own wishes and gain great merit in the eyes of God, as was the case in many of the battles Job endured. If you recall, it angered and frustrated Satan to no end because Job had used the pain and suffering to gain merit in God's sight. Satan eventually won in a particular battle because he utilized the influence of Job's friends. He caused Job to doubt and speak contemptuously to God. In effect, he caused Job and God's relationship to be widened instead of closed.

What is there that Satan doesn't want?

THE ONE THING THAT SATAN CERTAINLY DOESN'T WANT IS FOR MAN TO COME CLOSER TO GOD. This is dead against what he wants. And this is also the key to both getting Satan to stop sending you pain and suffering, and to gaining the greatest merit from the pain and suffering that you will still endure. Satan thinks that we will be angry at God for allowing this to happen, and that this anger will turn us against God and push us farther away from him. It doesn't have to! Here's how to turn the tables of this game on him to your own advantage.

RULE #2: WHENEVER ANY EVIL, PAIN, OR SUFFERING BEFALLS YOU, INSTEAD OF HAVING IT TURN YOU AWAY FROM GOD, LET IT TURN YOU TOWARD HIM AND MAKE YOUR LOVE FOR GOD PURER AND STRONGER.

And how do you do this?

Make a short offertory prayer, such as this one: "Oh, sweet Jesus, I offer You this (pain, suffering, inconvenience, trouble, temptation...) out of my love for You and my desire to love You better. I offer it in reparation for all of my sins and the sins of all men, and to Your greater glory and honor. Please use this to purify my love for You and repair the evil that I have done."

Man, you talk about upsetting Satan! This infuriates him. If you faithfully practice this every time that even the slightest little inconvenience befalls you, it won't be long before Satan is convinced that you will always do it. I've found that the result of applying these two rules in my own life has been the cessation of almost all pain and suffering. In addition, because Satan fears I will use whatever evil I am aware of to my benefit, he even hides much of the evil that happens around me from my mind.

Which should we do first, the offertory prayer or stop hurting others?

Both, and the key is the first ninety percent that we cause to ourselves. It doesn't do any good to attempt to offer any of it to God, because it's not kosher. If I hit myself in the foot with a hammer on purpose and then say, "Oh, God, I offer this pain to

You!" I think He wouldn't be very pleased or amused. So we have to overcome this first before we can apply the second rule.

The seminar is free, and I will give it to any individual or any group of people that will endure it. I wish you love, peace, and joy. Thank you for attending this workshop. May Dad put you in His favor and keep you there eternally. Bye!

CHAPTER 18
Life Is For Enjoying

God: Isn't life wonderful, Peniel?

Me: It is. It has been for me ever since I found the truth.

And what did you find to be the truth?

You! You are the only truth. Not only did I find the truth, I accepted the truth just as it is. I accept You just as You are. I love You.

And I feel naturally toward you also.

Sometimes life is so great that I can hardly contain myself. I just want to grab someone and kiss them. I wish that You and I could be in more intimate contact. I wish to hold You tightly and allow You to hug me. And I know that I can do this through holding those who love me—such as my sweet wife or wonderful daughter.

And I wish to be close to you. What father does not wish these things about his beloved children? And, in time, all things will be as you wish them—so long as you maintain your present love for Me. I have big plans for you.

What shall we talk about today?

<u>Life</u>. Tell Me, Peniel, what do you think life's purpose is?

I have an analogy for it that is one of the workshops titles. It is: **<u>Life Is For Enjoying</u>!**

Very good. That is a good analogy. Why is life for enjoying?

Because You are the life that we refer to when we say <u>life</u>. And You wish for us to enjoy You!

Why am I enjoyable?

Because You alone are truly good. Only what is good can be really enjoyed—and You are all that is good. Everything that is good is contained within You, created by You, and sustained by You.

Why have I created, contained, and sustained what I have?

Because it was your choice. You needed no reasons to do as You chose. It was good that You did it, and so You did it. You did it out of love—out of yourself, being that You **are** love.

What benefits or results come from the creation and sustaining of what was made?

You created the universe and sustain it. It is good and it is greatly enjoyed by mankind. It serves all our needs and gives us pleasure. It is held in existence for us to use and enjoy by You out of Your love for us. There is nothing that is good for us that You would not do, therefore You have done all the good that could be done for us.

Then why is mankind and the world in such a pitiful and troubled state?

Because, like spoiled and immature children, mankind in general has wasted, abused, misused, and maltreated the wonderful gifts of love that You provided for us. You do not force us to accept the wonderful love gifts that You have for us; we are free to refuse You and Your love. It is as if we were the children of a rich and powerful king who loved us completely.

Due to man's Fall, we seldom appreciate, use wisely, or enjoy all of the bountiful tools and gifts that You have provided for us. The good and the gifts remain unused, because of our stubborn refusal to accept them from You. If we are not filled with joy and excitement and all manner of good and positive emotions, it is not because You are unable or unwilling to give them to us. Rather it is due to our obstinate refusal to accept these wonderful treasures.

Why would one of you refuse My gifts of love or tools for your improvement?

Because our nature has been corrupted—we have become base and vain. We would rather rule in hell than serve or accept charity in heaven. These false beliefs have been with man since the Fall.

Why are such false beliefs so widespread among all people in the world?

Because we refuse to accept reason when it comes to us. And we refuse to look for wisdom where we know that it is. We become complacent and believe that the state that we are in is the best state that we could be in.

Do you not realize that things could be better? Do you not understand that there are things that you want and things about your life that you would change if you had the chance?

Yes, deep down we know all this. Yet we deny the fact to our conscious mind most of the time. And in an unguarded moment when these possibilities do surface within the confines of our conscious mind, we tell ourselves that this is just the way things are—it is the will of God that it be this way, it is our lot in life to suffer, we don't deserve any better—or some other such justification.

Why do you have to justify the way your life is at these times?

Because our lives are not as we should like to have them. And since they are not, we make excuses to ourselves so that we will believe that there is nothing that can be done to change the way things are.

And why do you need to believe there is nothing that can be done to improve your situation?

Because if we allowed the possibility that something could be done to improve our life, why aren't we doing it? We should have to justify our own inactivity and refusal to learn to ourselves. Better to stick our head in the sands of <u>I don't want to discuss this stuff</u> than to admit that we were mistaken in our beliefs.

Why is it so important that you believe your beliefs are correct?

Because most of us do not think that it is a matter of being correct or incorrect, which is the true case. Rather, we think it is a matter of being right or wrong. We will never, ever, admit that we are wrong, even if we really know that we are mistaken!

What then is the difference between being correct and being right?

In truth—and not as most people use the words—to be correct means to be in agreement with reality. If you have the answer "7" for the question "What is 2 X 3?" then your answer is incorrect—not wrong. If you slap an innocent child for no reason, you are WRONG, not incorrect. Correct and incorrect are not moral issues; they deal only with being in agreement with reality (what works). If what you believe is correct, then it will work. Correct and incorrect NEVER have to do with things of emotions or spirit (personality). Right and wrong have to do with moral or personal issues. Being right or wrong always has to do with emotional and spiritual things.

Here are some examples to illustrate the proper way that I believe these words should be used: It is correct that 2 X 3 equals 6. It is right to love your neighbor. It is incorrect to clean your car with sandpaper. It is wrong to take it out on your family because someone at work upset you. It is incorrect to believe that God is dead. It is wrong to refuse to accept God's loving gifts for us.

Basically, if it deals only with reason or reasonableness and has little or nothing to do with emotions or morality, then it is a question of correct or incorrect. If it has to do with morality, strong emotions, or what God likes or dislikes, then it is a question of right and wrong. It is right to love. It is wrong to be proud (except for holy pride in God and what good God has done in and through us; pride in God is good—pride in self is not). It is correct to be in agreement with the natural course and laws of the universe. It is incorrect to be out of harmony with the laws and ways of the universe. What is correct will work in the world. What is incorrect will not work in the world. Neither brings God's approval or disapproval upon you.

What is right is in agreement with the laws and desires of God. What is right will bring you well being in some form or another when it is adhered to or followed. (Such as the precept that giving your hat to someone that steals your coat, when followed because of the love for Christ, shall make you feel extremely good inside.) What is wrong is only that which goes against your conscience. It is against your true nature and brings with it guilt.

Guilt is the thing that causes us the most trouble and is most disturbing to our inner peace and calmness. We will do virtually anything to avoid guilt. This is why we have such a difficult time with accepting the truth when it seems to disagree with what is already within our belief system. We think that to see some new truth is to admit that our former beliefs (and therefore the life that we were living as a result of accepting these beliefs) are WRONG! In truth, it is not a question of being right or wrong, it is a question of being correct or incorrect. If the beliefs that you are operating from now are not in agreement with truth, then they are merely INCORRECT, not wrong. Yet, when they are questioned, we think that the other person is attempting to prove us wrong. And for us to admit that we were wrong would insinuate that we should have to feel guilty over having believed what was not in agreement with the truth. Therefore we are usually unwilling to see that our currently held beliefs are false. It is not that they are WRONG beliefs; it is just that they are FALSE beliefs. If they were truly wrong, then we should have to feel guilty over having lived by them. Since they are just false—incorrect, not in agreement with what is true, not in agreement with our own reason—it would be very easy to change them just as we do dirty socks that no longer are appealing to us.

If reason shows you that your current beliefs do not agree with your own reason, please do not think that you are WRONG, for you are not! You are only mistaken, as you have been mistaken when taking a math test in the past. There is no guilt involved in admitting that the answer that we had was not the true answer; we can correct it with easy grace. It doesn't cause us a conflict with our conscience or ego, for it is not an issue of emotions or guilt. There is no fear of making another error in math later, and we are fairly sure that we shall probably make other mistakes in the future regarding math. The important thing is to learn from our current mistake where we erred and strayed away from the reasonable path—or where the flaw in our logic was that led us to this incorrect answer. We wish to learn from this incorrectness how to be more consistently correct in the future—nothing more. There is no fear of being incorrect or making mistakes, for that will cause us no shame or guilt.

This is the way we must understand our belief system is, and accept and treat it in this way. If we continue to believe that our beliefs—if proved incorrect by reason or another person's logic—make us WRONG, then what chance have we given ourselves to find the real truth?

Imagine that if, in school, every time the teacher pointed out an error on your test answers (to help you to think more reasonably in the future) you took this as a personal insult and felt guilty about being WRONG. I don't think it would be long before you started having great difficulty. You would probably rather not discuss math at all and say, "I do not like to discuss math (religion, philosophy, morality, God, sin, theology, Satan, angels, love, personality... Take your pick!), because it usually leads to an argument." What you probably would mean instead is that you feared discussing <u>anything</u> because you were afraid that someone would prove you wrong (as they had done in the past) about this subject, and then you would feel guilty again. In order to keep them from winning (where you would have to accept their point of view over your own), you would probably have to resort to ignoring reason and allow your emotions to run your mouth and mind. That is why the discussion would turn into an argument. You would be unwilling to accept your own reason; to retain your own self-righteousness you would probably talk loud and become angry. You would feel like you were being attacked. You would run for the hills! You would far rather be RIGHT than to learn any truth!

Why?

Most people would rather be RIGHT than anything else. We would rather believe that we are Right than to learn the truth. We would rather be Right than to enjoy life and have all manner of good things. For some, being Right is even chosen over being alive!

How do you mean?

There are many people that commit suicide just to prove to everyone else that they were RIGHT! They leave a suicide note that says something like, "I told you guys how messed up my life was and what terrible suffering I had to endure. I told you that my life wasn't even worth living, and see—I was right. What a sacrifice I have made—JUST TO SHOW YOU ALL HOW RIGHT I WAS!" I believe that most suicides are the ultimate statement of, "See, I was RIGHT!"

This is a terrible thing, is it not?

Yes, the dire need to believe that we are in the Right—no matter what—is one reason so many of us will not learn. We do not change—our lives do not improve—because we refuse to admit that what we now believe is in error!

Surely a man who thinks that his life could be made richer and happier would be willing to change his beliefs if they were not true.

Yes, you would think that this would be the case for all men. Yet we have this terrible disease that prevents most of us from seeing the light.

And what is this disease called?

Pride. Pride is the only sin. All other sins are a result of this sin. It was the first sin, is now the biggest sin, and shall be our last sin.

Why?

Pride is why Lucifer became Satan. Pride is what instilled greed in Eve and pride is what led man to follow where the woman had gone. Pride is why we are taught so insistently that it is far better to be in the right (in our own minds) than to enjoy life or anything else. "TO BELIEVE THAT YOU ARE RIGHT is more important than all else—this is the secret to life!" This is what many of us are taught. This is why we can stand obstinately in tunnel #4 forever, without any cheese, ignoring anyone that might come along and say, "You know—I was just in tunnel #2 and there was quite a lot of cheese in that tunnel. It was delicious and I think maybe you ought to at least check it out." We will say, "I know that I am in the **right** tunnel. That is all that is important to me. I can do without cheese. SO LONG AS I KNOW THAT THIS IS THE RIGHT TUNNEL!"

So pride is man's greatest evil?

Yes. It is the root beneath the tree of evil. It supports the trunk of false beliefs and the giant limbs of Self-righteousness, Greed, Fear, and all manner of other evils that we have accepted.

And is it this way for all men?

No. There are those of us who have either been given the light or have had it shown to us. We may have been raised in darkness, and are not even aware that we are in the dark. If we have never experienced the light, we would not know that we were in the dark. Yet, we can always come to the light.

And what is the light?

Truth!

And what is the truth?

You are!

And where is the truth to be found?

Within ourselves. This is where You reside most intensely.

Can I be found in others also?

Your presence may be recognized in others—if we will allow ourselves to lower the walls of fear to look out of our fort of self-righteousness. We will recognize Your intense presence in others because they have lots of cheese. They are happy and fun-loving, enjoying life tremendously. And they have that one big hunk of cheese that we really hunger for more than all things.

And what is that?

Peace of mind. It is also called by many other names, such as fulfillment and tranquility.

And is this the best of things to have as a human being?

There is no better thing. For if you are rich, and have no peace of mind, you will detest yourself and your life, and you will want rather things to be different. If you are beautiful, and have no peace of mind, you will not allow yourself to really enjoy the compliments of others, and you will want things to be different. If you are healthy and strong, and you have no peace of mind, you will not be content and you want things to be different.

How can peace of mind be acquired?

It cannot be bought or purchased, or stolen or found.

Then where can a person get it?

He may only receive it from You, if You are willing to give it to him.

And what would make Me willing to give it to a person?

If that person was to dedicate himself to the truth and sincerely seek the truth, then You would show him the truth; and if he accepts all of the truth that You wish to send to him, You will also give him the peace of mind that comes from wisdom.

And what wisdom brings this peace of mind?

The wisdom that You are who You are, and that we are Your beloved children. The wisdom that we have done all that we should do and that we are now pleasing to You.

How can a person be sure of this?

Because of the sign of fulfillment in his life.

And what is the sign of fulfillment?

That a person has qualities very similar to You, Yourself. If they have become their natural self, and they were created in Your image, then when they once again become their true self, many of Your attributes will be apparent in their personalities.

And what are some of these attributes?

They are without want. They do not want for anything because there is nothing that they lack for their complete perfection. There is nothing about themselves or their lives that they would change because it is as it was intended by You to be, so they would not change anything even if they could. This is called fulfillment.

They are very happy and they truly enjoy life as is natural for a person. They are like a little kid in this respect. They are full of the sense of wonder over the universe and all of its mysteries. They have achieved perfection. They are as they were intended to be. They have achieved Nirvana, which is characterized by success, well-being, and good fortune (as was discussed earlier). All that Nirvana brings, they have.

Their life is a life virtually free of sin and guilt. They are honest with themselves and others. They have no need to feel that they are RIGHT because they now have so much cheese! LIFE BECOMES AS LIFE WAS INTENDED TO BE FOR THEM—they really start to enjoy it.

Life Is For Enjoying! And only our own pride and refusal to accept the truth and live our lives with truth is stopping most of us from enjoying life!

Very good. All that you have stated here is good and useful to those of My children who shall read this with an open mind and thirst for truth.

And now let us speak of life as it is for those who have accepted Me and have accepted all the truth as it is. Tell Me of life lived naturally in this perfected state.

Oh, sweet Jesus, my life—as it has been for some time now—is beyond description! Words cannot possibly convey the depth of peace and joy that You have allowed me to share with You. You have done things for me that only You can understand. Yet I feel that it is good that I attempt to describe, in whatever words that I may find to fit, this wondrous state that my soul is in.

Understand two things, reader: One, this life is an interior life in general, so many who see me in the world will see only a fraction of these wonderful things that are here inside of my interior castles. What they will see is only the slight reflection of the joy and peace that is within. And two, attempting to describe these things to someone who is not enlightened is like attempting to describe the feelings and emotions of making love to a person who has not experienced it for themselves. Life is marvelous!

Describe, as best you can, how the natural life is. Describe to them the way that your life has been since you came to know Me well and accepted Me just as I am. Tell how you think and feel; perhaps this will draw some towards this life.

I shall do my best.

Reader, remember back to the life you had as a child. Think of all of the joy that you had and the excitement that pervaded Your life. You had this excited joy because you were always anticipating some new goal that you thought was wonderful and enjoyable. You'd say, "I just can't wait until 3 P.M., because then school will be out and I can run and play baseball. I just can't wait until Saturday because I'm going fishing with dad. I just can't wait until next month because school will be out and we will go on our vacation to the mountains. I just can't wait..." And as a happy and excited-over-life child there was always another "I just can't wait..."

What is there in your life now that you have this eager and excited anticipation over? If you are like most of the unenlightened people I know, there is very little—if anything—that you are excitedly awaiting in your life.

Your life can be changed, I assure you. But only through accepting and applying of truth can you again return to your natural state. The natural life is a most wondrous life. What joy to love God purely, to love yourself and everything about yourself and your life! What ecstasy to know Jesus as a real and alive person in your everyday life. What a pleasure to walk casually with Him in all things and to speak with Him at will!

The natural life is much like the life that a happy child enjoys. It is full of wonder and excitement, joy and peace. Contentment and the absence of worry are two of the hallmarks of this type of life. What did you worry about when you were out playing in the mud? What disturbed your peace when you were fishing for perch on the boat? The reason that your life was so carefree is that you knew that dad was there to take care of all of the problems that might arise. If your line got caught in a tree, he'd stop fishing and get it for you. You knew that he cared more about assisting you to have a good time than catching a lot of fish.

This is just as it is in the natural life that I keep speaking of. You have returned to the natural qualities that an innocent child has. Qualities such as peace, joy, excitement in everyday life, and enjoyment of even the simplest of things. And your true Father, the perfect loving Father, will be as close and as present in your life as you will allow Him to be. If you allow Him to walk with you each step of the way, each moment of the day, then this He will do. What more could a loving father want than to be by the side of his beloved and loving child all day long as his sweet child goes about his everyday business.

To be there and to share all of the joy—that is what fellowship with the Father is really about. To allow Him into your life to walk beside you—that is the height of joy in life. For if He be beside you, what would you fear? If He holds you near and dear to Him, what evil may befall you? If your Father was right there at all times, what beauty that He has made for you would He not point out to you and say, "See how much I love you! I have even made this for your pleasure and enjoyment." If He stood beside you in the times of trouble what enemy would you fear? If He stood beside you in all things, your joy would be doubled for it would be shared with Him. Your sorrow would be halved, for your understanding Father would bear you through it with tender mercy. Your way would be made clear, for He is the true way.

There would be no dark in your soul, for He would reside there; and where He is, there also is the true light that lights the minds of men. There would be no distress, for He is the comforter. There would be no desiring, for He is the object of man's desiring. There would be no trouble, for He is our refuge. There would be no problems, for He is the solver of tribulations. There would be no pain, for He is the healer. There would be no discord, for He is the bringer of harmony. There would be no guilt, for He is the forgiver of sins. There would be no evil, for He is the only good and all good. There would be no distress, for He is the prince of peace. There would be no incompetence, for He is the giver of power. There would be no death, for He is the very life that we have.

There would be no bad or evil or negative thing, for these things are all in opposition to Him. If the light comes into the room, shall the darkness say, "I shall stick around and visit for a while?" No, for there can be no darkness where there is pure light. And Jesus is the purest of all light. Shall the weak throw the strong out of their own house? No, and all power in heaven and on earth has been given to Him. Shall the evil destroy or defeat the good? No, for even though evil sometimes appears to have gotten the better of you, it is not possible so long as you persist to remain true to God and in His favor. Evil may torment you when he thinks that he has won and has the upper hand (such as when Satan succeeded in having the Son Of God murdered by the leaders of God's own chosen people).

Yet He that is perfectly good shall turn others' evil plans to good for you. Evil shall laugh and say, "I have won!" and he may dance around at your trouble and suffering, but very soon the almighty Father shall turn it to your advantage. And then you shall say, "Oh, evil, where is your laughter? Why do you weep and gnash your teeth? Where is the evil that you thought you were doing to me"?

And God shall reward you mightily for all that you willingly endured at the hands of those that saw not the light. You shall rejoice in your troubles and tribulations as well as the pleasure and good times. If your life be such, what could stop you from accomplishing anything? All that you must do is to accept that you are not now as you wish to be, and then find the way to return to yourself.

If you do not know the way and if it be your wish, **I shall assist you in any way that I can, for this is my mission in life.** If you choose not to be led by me, then I beg of you, find some good spiritual director to lead you in your beginning steps. Please do not follow the dangerous path that I did through my ignorance. I decided to do it all on my own for I was too proud to accept the advice of any spiritual counselor for a long while. I did not realize then that the evil forces know full well who might become a serious threat to them in the near future. They will set many traps to destroy you before you achieve the necessary wisdom to defend yourself from them. It is not enough to trust in God and then jump off a cliff simply because you are looking for the fastest way down the mountain. God may not be amused at your testing of Him. He does not appreciate it when one of His children jumps out of a tree just to see if He will catch them.

These are just a few of the terrible mistakes I made when I first started my pilgrimage inward. If it were not for the tender mercy and grace of God towards someone as foolish as myself, the evil that befell me would surely have overcome me and I would have wound up with ten times the troubles as I previously had. The trickery of Satan and his demons is very powerful and appealing to an innocent babe in Christ, and anyone who is just staring a serious calling to a devout life runs the terrible risk of being trampled by the mobs of demons that shall be sent to destroy or turn them away. It is far better to not start upon this journey than to start upon it insincerely or without the proper guidance to prevent being overwhelmed by the evil that shall surely be thrown at you.

Satan is little concerned with most people in their normal lives, for they do not seriously threaten his concerns. Yet one who receives a serious calling to the life of love and service to God he sees as a tremendous threat and one who may do him much damage. He will attack relentlessly and skillfully in the bewildering array of manifest tricks that he is allowed to utilize.

Please do not risk it. Find some dedicated servant of God, and ask him to be your spiritual adviser and guide along your path. But be cautious in selecting your guide. He or she should be a person with great love for God. Do not find someone who just appeals to your ego and tickles your ears. Rather, find the wisest person you can that is willing to assist you. Detachment and an objective mind are important qualities in a spiritual advisor. Test them by asking them about a difficult matter concerning spiritual things to assure yourself that they are wise in the ways of the spirit. Any wise man will understand that you should test his wisdom before submitting to his instructions.

And once you have accepted a counselor, be fully prepared to act according to his guidance rather than upon you own judgment.

Very, very good.

This is plenty for now. I am sure that many shall read this and come to understand that there may be a better life awaiting them when they seriously decide to accept it from Me. I am deeply pleased at your ability to express the joy that life with Me can bring. You are getting much better at conveying these things, My son. I love you more than you can know!

And I love You with all my heart, soul, mind, and strength—Dad.

CHAPTER 19
The Word

Me: Hello, Dad.

God: Hello, Peniel.

What shall we talk about now?

The Word.

Which one?

THE Word!

Oh, You.

Yes. I AM the Word. I am the way, the truth, and the light. I am the Father's Word.

All right. Can we cover the opening of John?

Sure.

I'll recount it here:

JOHN: 1

1 In the beginning was the Word, and the Word was with God, and the Word was God.

2 He was in the beginning with God.

3 All things were made through Him, and without Him nothing was made that was made.

4 In Him was life, and the life was the light of men.

5 And the light shines in the darkness, and the darkness did not comprehend it.

6 There was a man sent from God, whose name was John.

7 This man came for a witness, to bear witness of the Light, that all through Him might believe.

8 He was not that Light, but was sent to bear witness of that Light.

9 That was the true Light which gives Light to every man who comes into the world.

10 He was in the world, and the world was made through Him, and the world did not know Him.

11 He came to His own, and His own did not receive Him.

12 But as many as received Him, to them He gave the power to become children of God, even to those who believe in His name:

13 who were born, not of blood, nor of the will of the flesh, nor of the will of man, but of God.

14 And the Word became flesh and dwelt among us, and we beheld His glory, the glory as of the only begotten of the Father, full of grace and truth.

Okay, this is the Word that I was referring to. I am the Word. When John opened his gospel, he told of Me.

Let's see how much you have learned about Me. Tell Me as best you can what all of this means.

I shall; yet, it will probably take a long time to cover it in depth as I have learned it.

I'm not going anywhere. Take all the time you wish. If it goes on and on, then just quit where you wish to.

It is very difficult to put any of this into words correctly—although the understanding of all of this is very clear in the inner concepts of my mind. I wish that I could convey it to the reader in pure concepts, as Jesus does with the things He reveals to me. But this is a book, so I shall do the best I can with what I have.

I can see that it would take a thousand pages to even begin to convey the simplest of concepts that are so vividly and clearly contained within my mind's eyes. I shall just have to speak in the terms that fit best and leave some readers lost—for there are no better words to convey this.

If some of this loses you, dear reader, reread it and try and see it from a different point of view. It would be much easier to express if I could be with you and you could hear the expressions and nuances of tone and speech that are not contained here. Yet this is the best I can do in a book. Remember, all of this is simply my own opinion. I cannot vouch for the truth of any of it—so please take it with reservations.

I'll do the explanation a verse at a time.

Verse 1: "In the beginning was the Word, and the Word was with God, and the Word was God." In the beginning refers to the period before time. I originally said, "refers to the time before time," but then I realized that this is an absurd statement. How could it be a time before time? So I changed it to the word period instead. Our words do not work well when dealing with these things, but I have to use them as best I can to convey what I mean.

Time started when the physical universe was created—for time is the measure of physical change. Before the universe was created, there was no physical thing, therefore, there was no change—there was no time. The only thing we can say about any existence prior to the beginning of time starting at the creation of the universe is that it was before time, or In the beginning. So, In the beginning refers to existence as it was before time—before the creation of the universe.

What was there before time? Well, if all things were created, and before they were created there was nothing created; then, before creation, there was the uncreated. This is a paraphrasing of part of verse 1.

In the beginning means before time—before creation. In the beginning was the Word. Now, what does was the Word mean? Well, was means that it had existence and was real. Was is past tense, meaning that it was this way before now. And this means that the Word had existence and was real and this was prior to the present.

The Word is the most important part of this opening statement. Why refer to Him as the Word? Why not say, "In the beginning was God and His kid"? Well, there is an obvious reason for referring to the Son of God as the Word. It is illustrated by different and subtle meanings of the word Word. I shall not cover all of them here. I shall give a couple of their meanings and leave it to the reader to make the connections and gestalts with truth.

What does word mean to us? In our terms it means something that is expressed (or said). But it is deeper than this. For instance, it refers to a speech sound that symbolizes and communicates a meaning without being divisible into smaller parts capable of being understood the same way. It also refers to the expressed manifestation of the will and concept of the mind communicated in a means comprehensible to the recipient of the message being conveyed. And, it also means assurance, as in, "I give you my word." A man's word is sacred. And God's **Word** is not only sacred, it is Holy and Personal.

This is how I have learned it.

God the Father **is** existence, the foundation, the uncreated, He who was, is, and shall be. Before time, He was. He has a nature that was triune, for He was a spirit.

His nature, as the Father, is epitomized by existence itself. What makes the Father different from all else is that contained within His very essence and nature is the reason and force of His own existence. Hence, He alone is the uncreated source. None other has within their own personal nature the reason and sustenance for their own existence. All others were either begotten or created. Without the Father to give existence to a thing and continuously sustain its existence, it would cease to be.

So, the Father is existence. He is the source. He is the only uncreated. By definition, we could not have two different Fathers, for if there were two sources, they could not be exactly the same. Two spirits that are exactly alike in every respect are one spirit. For there to have been two original sources (two distinctly different Gods) one of them would have had to contain some characteristic or ability that the other one lacked—or else they would be the same. Since one of them would have to be lacking in some quality, he could not be the perfect, complete being that we know God the Father (the Source) must be. Therefore, he would not have been God. There can be only one God, by the definition of God as being the complete, infinite, uncreated source of all that is (the Creator).

To further understand the Word, we must touch upon the type of nature that He has. His nature is the same as the nature of the Father, since they are two distinct persons in ONE nature. And both of Them have a Spiritual nature. So, I shall examine what I believe it means to have a spiritual nature.

Spirit is that which has true eternal existence (whether created or uncreated), has reasonable comprehension of its own existence by way of mental capacity (a fancy way of saying knows that it exists by thinking and conceiving this concept), and has the capability to love, convey love, and express love. (Remember, love takes care of needs and/or gives pleasure. It also can feel love for something that is good yet cannot be loved directly.) Therefore, in simpler form, spirit is, knows that it is, and can love. This is kinda like comparing the threefold nature of man. Man has a personality (his existence—the Father). Man also has a reasoning mind (his comprehension—the Son [or Word]). And lastly, man has his ability to love and receive love (his emotions—the Spirit). So, man is a real live being, reasonable in mind and emotional in nature.

Now, we are dealing primarily with the second part here. In our analogy, the Word is similar to man's ability to conceive. Mind is a good word for it. (No pun intended.) So the Word of God is the mind of God. His thoughts, concepts, understanding, and the expression of these would be a Word. Oh yes, being that it is God expressing this concept (thought, Word), it will be a very powerful, beautiful and complete Word. And what was there in the beginning for God to express in a Word? All that was to be created was created through His Word. As of then, nothing had been created. There was nothing in existence save God alone. His Word could therefore express but one thing alone—Himself. God formed a perfect, infinitely intense, and perfectly clear concept of Himself. The very forming of this thought begat His mind into existence. And His mind and this thought were both in His mind and were His mind. The thought was thought with infinite power and clarity, and it was totally complete and single-minded of purpose. This thought was then spoken (for lack of a clearer word to express it) from the mouth of God. The Word was said, and the Word became personal. The Word, being infinite in power, took on its own personality and was existent by the power of God (called the Father to distinguish Him from the Word—His Son, Jesus Christ, the Savior of mankind and Lord of all).

The Word of God is not a Word that is different in nature from the Father. Just as your words are not. Your words are not different from the nature of your personality, for it is the very nature of your personality that formed and conceived this word that you spoke. If anything, it is one in nature with your personality. It is not the same as your personality, for it has a different function than your personality. Your word could not exist if it were not for your personality existing prior to it and giving it form and power. And the word that a man speaks has great power if he speaks the truth and with great force of mind.

Imagine then, how powerful the eternal Word of the infinite Father must be. The purpose of the word that you speak is to express your personality in a means that the recipient of your communication may comprehend. If you knew that the recipient of your thought could only understand concepts given very slowly, then you would express Your concept in a word that may be limited from what you wished it to be.

But this is not the case for the Father's Word. He was the intended recipient of His own thought spoken as His Word. He is infinite in comprehension and understanding, so He expressed His Word in the most complete and perfect way, without limitation. He begat His Word, and the Word was God. And the Word was with God. Therefore, before time, God the Father formed and begat the Word, and the Word became a person separate and individual from the Father, yet with the same nature. There was God the Father, and His Son, the Word of God. And they were together in the beginning. They embraced in an embrace of perfect and pure and infinite love—and this Love was breathed forth from

Them and, being infinite, the Love became personal. The Love that the Father and Son shared in perfect harmony proceeds from the Father and the Son. The spirit of God is this spirit of Love that is formed of the emotions that the Father and the Son each have towards the other. The spirit of God is Love. God is a spirit, so God is Love!

I know that a few of you will be scratching your heads and muttering here—I'm sorry.

So, the Father begat and continuously begets the Son, His Word, His mind, His thought. It's kinda like saying that your personality continuously creates your mind, and your mind constantly allows you to conceive of your self (personality). In better terms, the power of God is contained within the Word of God. God's Word is where His power resides and is channeled. All of the power of God is channeled through His Word. All things are created through the Word. All that is, came through the Word of God. The Word of God made the world.

The second part of the first verse says, "and the Word was with God." It says and because it stresses the fact that They are distinct and that the Word was with God. The word with here doesn't represent location or proximity, for there was no physical universe yet. It represents the meaning of the word with as it is used in the sentence, "Don't worry, the whole team is with you!" It means of one mind, will, and accord.

The third part of the first verse says, "and the Word was God." The Word was God because He was one in being with the Father. Both of them have the same nature. Remember that God is merely a title that means Extremely Goooood and therefore both the Father and the Son were God. The Word was God. (i.e., He was Extremely Goooood!)

Verse 2 says, "He was in the beginning with God." The stress here is upon the fact that not only was the Word with God, He was with Him in the beginning. I will paraphrase this verse: "The Word of God was, before time, of the same will as God."

Verse 3 says, "All things were made through Him, and without Him nothing was made that was made." After the beginning was the creation. The creation was performed through the mind and power of God, the equivalent of saying "God's Word." Stress is laid here upon the fact that there is nothing in existence that came outside the result of the Father through the Word. Some may propose that God created some things but there may be things that were not created by the WORD. Here, that proposal is countered. All things were made by the Word, and without Him, nothing was made that is in existence.

Verse 4 says, "In Him was life, and the life was the light of men." That's going to get a little sticky explaining in human terms. For each part of this statement there are several possible meanings, and most of those meanings are correct (at least in part). In Him was life means that He was truly alive. It also means that life itself was contained within Him. Life, being considered as a force or essence, was in the Word. He was the life. The Word of God is the life of men. God's power is the power of life. Only within the mind of God is the true life. And about a hundred other paraphrasing that could shed extra meaning upon all that is meant in this statement. I leave this to you, the reader.

...and the life was the light of men. Light here is not the same as photons, even though the representation is similar for obvious reasons. It is the light referred to when you say, "I reread the passage and then the light of its meaning finally struck me." Light here means truth or revelation, or knowledge and wisdom. If you stop and consider the fundamentals of any type of life as technology has revealed it to us, you will see that even the simplest of life form's essence (that which causes it to be alive rather than not) is probably at the pinnacle of achievements of mind. Man could not even begin to create the DNA chains and the proper coding necessary for even the most basic of life forms. But just think: with the assistance of some protein molecules and acids arranged in a particular way, a creature has the ability to eat, breathe, grow, reproduce and pass on its genetic code.

Can you imagine the amount of information that it would require if man tried to have a computer do something even remotely similar to this? To have the computer accept parts of its surroundings into itself and utilize these foreign elements for its own advancement—it boggles the mind to even try and imagine how to even start such a program. This life that He refers to here is surely from the knowledge and wisdom of the Mind of God. And life is the light of men.

A second thing that this passage, and the life was the light of men, refers to is the life of Jesus. Before man had the opportunity to observe God Himself, in human form through the life of Jesus Christ, man was very much in the dark about the truth. And the truth that is most important is the answer to "What is God really like and why are we here?" These were some of the truths that Jesus' life shone into the minds of all men. Through Him, man was enlightened as to the truth about the nature and will of God. The light of men, the light that should guide all men in their walk, was the life of Christ.

Verse 5 says, "And the light shines in the darkness, and the darkness did not comprehend it." The light shines in the darkness and the darkness did not comprehend it. Notice that there are two different tenses used. The light shone in the darkness and is still shining even now. The darkness can and probably does represent many things: the ignorance of man, unenlightened persons, Satan and his forces, and the world in general (since it was under the rule of the Prince of Darkness, it was in the dark). If the darkness part of this is understood, then the rest of this statement is fairly easy. We could paraphrase this in many possible ways: "The Truth came into the world and none understood it." "The energy conservation expert came to assist the family to save money on their electric bill. When he got there, the lights were all on, the doors and windows were all wide open, the air conditioner was on high—and no one was home!" "Man, in his evil nature at that time, attempting to grasp the pure and glorious truth of Jesus, is like a blind man in a dark room looking for a black cat that isn't there."

Verse 6 says, "There was a man sent from God, whose name was John." and I shall only say that John was Elijah come again. Elijah had gone to be with God—and now came back to announce the coming Light. He came from God. I hope you have a blast with this one.

Verse 7 is self-explanatory: "This man came for a witness, to bear witness of the Light, that all through him might believe."

Verse 8 is, "He was not that Light, but was sent to bear witness of that Light." Once the light is understood, this is fairly easy also.

Verse 9 says, "That was the true Light which gives Light to every man who comes into the world." Hmmm. The Word of God gives every man who comes into the world the light. If every man is given the light, perhaps it is just that many do not comprehend the light?

Verse 10 says, "He was in the world, and the world was made through Him, and the world did not know Him." Pretty ironic, huh? The world here refers not to physical things such as rocks and trees, for they could not know Him. It refers to mankind and all of the sensible beings that are represented by the world. Paraphrased, this is, "Your Dad came to visit you and you didn't even recognize that He was your Dad."

Verse 11 says, "He came to His own, and His own did not receive Him." God's own chosen people did not accept the Messiah when He came for them.

Verse 12 says, "But as many as received Him, to them He gave the power to become children of God, even to those who believe in His name." This says that to those who did accept Him just as He was, He gave the power to become the children of God, or, as He says, "His brothers and sisters."

Verse 13 says, "who were born, not of blood, nor of the will of the flesh, nor of the will of man, but of God." I won't get into all this here, as this is a discussion on the Word of God.

Now, verse 14 says, "And the Word became flesh and dwelt among us, and we beheld His glory, the glory as of the only begotten of the Father, full of grace and truth." Think of this—all that I said that the Word represents became flesh and dwelt among us.

The Word is the power and truth. The Word is the light and life. In God's Word, we move and breathe and live. Because of God's Word, we may have life, and have it more abundantly. God keeps His Word; when God gives us His Word, you know that His

Word is as good as good itself is. God doesn't send His Word lightly, for His Word is a rare thing indeed. And what is more beautiful or noble than the Word of God? God's Word is the guidance and rudder of my life. If not for God's Word, I should be lost and forever condemned to eternal separation from my goal.

I live for God's Word, and nothing else can truly sate my soul's appetite. If I live, yet do not know the Word of God, of what purpose is my life? Man does not live by bread alone, but by the very Word that proceeds from the mouth of God. The Word Himself is the author of His Word. He Who Is wrote His Own Word, and spoke that Word. That Word is my rock and my salvation. It is as if God had finally said to suffering and evil man, "I give you my Word and My Word shall be true. To whoever shall receive My Word, just as It is, I shall give him the power to become My Child. It is out of My Love, My very Spirit, that I give My Word to you. After you have received My Word, and when My Word returns to Me again, then I shall send unto you the Spirit of the Word. That spirit gives life eternal, for that Spirit is the Holy Spirit, My Spirit, LOVE!"

...

Well, after having just read much of this chapter, it appears that my words are insufficient to convey my clear and concise understanding of this passage. What I have written here may seem vague and disjointed to you. Let me see if I can restate the concept of "The Word" in a more simplistic set of terms.

To me, the Word is love, family, life—**one**.

Very good, Peniel. You have indeed come a long way. I know all that was in your mind and I understand that you know the truth far better than can be expressed in words. You did a good job of conveying some of it well.

CHAPTER 20

Love, One More Time!

Me: Well, here we are at the last conversation in this book.

God: Yes.

How do You want to finish these conversations off? We have talked about so many wonderful things.

Yes. We have covered a couple of the relevant subjects, and yet we could make a thousand books like this one and not cover all of the wonderful things that we have already talked about over the years.

I know. You have shown me so much—I am deeply grateful for all of the wisdom and tools that You have bestowed upon me. Thanks.

You're very welcome. Thank you for taking the time to listen to Me. I appreciate all the sacrifices that you have made in order to bring yourself to this stage of mental and spiritual development. You have achieved much, Peniel.

I only hope that it will do as much good as it can. This is my only wish. I dedicate and offer all the things that I do to You, Dad. I offer it all to the Greater Glory of God! I love You.

And I love you!

Let's speak of love again! I think that it is only fitting to begin and end this book with the highest truth of all: Love.

Super. After all, Love is both Your and my favorite subject. There is nothing so wonderful, so good, yet so misunderstood, as love. If we humans could only learn to treat others with love, our lives and the state of the world in general would be so improved. I pray for this, although I am fully aware that prophecy says that things will probably not turn out this way for some time yet.

What then can a person do to make the best of what I have given him or her?

They can do the best they can. If a person just achieved a small part of his or her full potential, they would probably be far greater than they now are allowing themselves to be. Who among those that read this can honestly say that in the important things in life, they are very close to their full potential?

And what, Peniel, are the important things in life?

To be in a good, close, loving relationship with God. To do as God intended us to do. To be as close to all that we can be—as we are capable of being at the present time. To love all that is good with a pure and contrite heart. To see good where good is and to not refuse to appreciate good that is sent to us. To receive the love of God in an easy and casual way. To lovingly accept all of the gifts and care that God wishes for us. To follow the precepts and commandments of God. In other words, to be our natural self.

And what are the main precepts that I wish for My children to follow?

To love You through loving our neighbor as best we can. To accept all that You send for us. To give with a willing heart. To receive with joy. To live with peace in our minds and hearts. To appreciate and not abuse the miracles of nature. To understand life's essential elements.

Oh, you're on a roll. And what are life's essential elements?

Truth, love, joy, peace of mind, fairness, acceptance, and forgiveness, and anything and everything else that was shown as the example to follow.

And where is this example to be found?

In the life of Christ. You came, in part, to give us the example of what God would wish for our lives to be like. We would be very wise indeed to accept this wonderful example, and guide our lives by the infallible precepts that You revealed through Your life.

Good. And what else should a person do?

Understand the answer to all of their and mankind's problems.

What is the answer to all of these different problems?

Love is the answer. You alone can solve the problems of our day-to-day life, or the big problems of the world in general.

Why do I not come into a person's life and solve their problems?

Many do not ask You to. Many do not believe that You can, should, or will. I feel very sorry for them.

What else would you add, since this is the closing of the book and will be the last opportunity to relay your message to the readers of this book?

My dear friends, I only wish that the true peace of mind that I have received was yours also. For if you are rich, and have not peace of mind, you shall hate your wealth. If you are handsome, and fear death, you shall not enjoy your life. Peace of mind is the most important thing for a person to have in his or her life—and true peace of mind comes only from the sure knowledge that your life is as it was intended to be. When you can honestly say, "I wouldn't change a thing!" then you shall have true peace of mind.

Are there other things that are necessary to achieve peace of mind?

You cannot achieve peace of mind; it comes only as the gift of the Father.

Then how shall a person receive peace of mind?

Become what God wishes of you—then He shall freely give it to you.

What does God wish of you?

To be your natural, joyous, loving self.

How shall a person become himself?

By returning back to the self he was as a happy child—for such is the kingdom of heaven. You shall not enter the kingdom unless you become as one of these innocent and loving children.

How can a person return to his natural self?

Backtrack over the way you have come.

Can a person do this without guidance?

Perhaps, yet I wouldn't attempt it if a guide was available for free.

Who should guide a person?

God should.

And will God?

What father would not willingly assist his child back home? Yes, God would—if we would or could allow Him to.

Why doesn't this happen more often?

For most of us, by the time we make the sincere decision to return to our natural self, we cannot then hear or perceive the subtle nuances of God's guiding spirit within us. And Satan is a powerful and crafty foe. It is a path with many dangers to him who is unaware.

How then should a person go?

Find a wise counselor for your journey and test him or her to be sure that you have gotten what you want as a guide. Do not be titillated by a guide that tickles your ears with promises of great heights in short order. Rather, be thrifty in selecting your guide on this most important journey inward. The best guide is the detached and wise guide who is more concerned with the ability to love God and neighbor more purely than to achieve great heights of mental or spiritual development. Do not allow your ego to be your guide, rather, allow your heart to guide you.

And where is a guide such as this to be found?

I wish I could tell you. If you are sincere and you ask God to assist you to find the guide that He intends for you, He shall surely show you the way to proceed. If you can find no other, I offer my assistance to the sincere seeker of Truth. Yet God has many other plans for me. He knows best. Ask Him for His guidance and then follow what your heart tells you is right and reasonable.

Very good, Peniel. Indeed, I shall guide those who may hear Me. And for those who will not hear Me, I shall surely help them to understand how they may best find the truth. If you are sincere about becoming all that I wish for you to be, I shall surely show you how to start. What kind of Father would I be if I didn't put forth great effort to at least show you where to find your guide, since you cannot yet hear Me? This is the main reason I had Peniel write this book!

Nothing is more important than the return of one of My wayward sheep to the fold. There is more rejoicing in heaven over one repentant sinner than over all of the great works of any good man. For the return of a lost sheep is like unto the birth of a new child in the kingdom of God. My heart is filled with great joy when one of My children who has been led astray returns to the light.

Please, I ask of you, return to the joy and peace that life offers you. Do the will of God and seek Me first—and all other things shall be added to you.

Beautiful.

And now let's talk about love.

One last time, Peniel—what is Love?

Love is God. God is Love.

Is love an emotion?

No. Love causes all emotions. Love is a Person. You are that Person.

What is the personality of love like?

I shall quote here some of the things that have been said about Love. I have set down some selected passages from various sources, and then I have rephrased some of them substituting some of the parallel meanings for the words Love, and God, and others. I hope they shed a little light on this most wonderful subject for you. Read them carefully and glean all that they contain. I honestly hope that some of this shall sink deep into your mind and assist you in your decision about love.

SELECTED LOVE PASSAGES

1. Love only takes care of needs and gives pleasure.

   God only takes care of needs and gives pleasure.

2. Love only has one need—to be expressed.

   God only has one need—to be expressed.

3. If Love's need is not met by you, Love shall leave you.

   If God's need is not met by you, God shall leave you.

4. Only that which is good can be truly loved.

   Only that which is God can be truly loved.

5. Love's only enemies are fear and ignorance of Love.

   God's only enemies are fear and ignorance of God.

6. Whenever you take care of another's needs or give them pleasure selflessly, you are showing them Love.

   Whenever you take care of another's needs or give them pleasure selflessly, you are showing them God.

7. What is good must be Loved, lest Love shall leave you cold.

   What is good must be God, lest God shall leave you cold.

8. Refusal to love what is good results in a loss of peace and joy.

   Refusal to feel and act as God Himself does toward what is good results in a loss of peace and joy.

9. If Love comes to you, do not think that you may direct Love's course. For if Love finds you worthy, He will direct your course.

If God comes to you, do not think that you may direct God's course. For if God finds you worthy, He will direct your course.

10. Love is not reasonable. It is beyond the realms of mere reason.

To feel and act as God Himself does toward another is not reasonable. It is beyond the realms of mere reason.

11. If you say, "I love you because…" then you deceive yourself.

If you say, "I feel and act as God Himself does toward you because…" then you deceive yourself.

12. Love is very patient and kind, never jealous or envious, never boastful or proud, never haughty or selfish or rude. Love does not demand its own way. Love is not irritable or touchy. Love does not hold grudges and will hardly even notice when others do Love wrong. Love is never glad about injustice, but rejoices whenever truth wins out. If you love someone you will be loyal to him or her no matter what the cost. You will always believe in them, always expect the best of them, and always stand your ground in defending them.

God is very patient and kind, never jealous or envious, never boastful or proud, never haughty or selfish or rude. God does not demand His own way. God is not irritable or touchy. God does not hold grudges and will hardly even notice when others do Him wrong. God is never glad about injustice, but rejoices whenever truth wins out. If you feel and act as God Himself does toward someone you will be loyal to them no matter what the cost. You will always believe in them, always expect the best of them, and always stand your ground in defending them.

13. (Jesus) Little children, I shall be with you a little while longer. You will seek Me; and as I said to the Jews, "Where I am going, you cannot come." So now I say to you, "A new commandment I give to you, THAT YOU LOVE ONE ANOTHER; as I have loved you, that you also love one another."

Little children, Love shall be with you a little while longer. You will seek Love; and as I said to the Jews, "Where Love is going, you cannot come." So now Love says to you, "A new commandment Love gives to you, THAT YOU FEEL AND ACT AS GOD HIMSELF DOES TOWARD ONE ANOTHER; as I have felt and acted as God Himself did toward you, that you also feel and act as God Himself does toward one another."

14. (Jesus) By this all will know that you are My disciples, if you have love for one another.

By this all will know that you are My disciples, if you feel and act as God Himself does toward one another.

15. (Jesus) He who has My commandments and keeps them, is he who loves Me. And he who loves Me shall be loved by My Father, and I will love him and manifest Myself to him.

He who has My commandments and keeps them, is he who feels and acts as God Himself does towards Me. And he who feels and acts as God does towards Me shall be loved by My Father, and I will love him and manifest Myself to him.

16. (Jesus) If anyone loves Me, he will keep My word; and My Father will love him, and We will come to him and make Our home with him. He who does not love Me does not keep My words; and the word which you hear is not Mine; but the Father's who sent Me.

If anyone feels and acts as God Himself does toward Me, he will keep My word; and My Father will love him, and We will come to him and make Our home with him. He who does not feel and act as God Himself does toward Me does not keep My words; and the word which you hear is not Mine; but the Father's who sent Me.

17. (Jesus) As the Father loved Me, I also have loved you; abide in My love. If you keep My commandments, you will abide in My love, just as I have kept My Father's commandments and abide in His love. These things I have spoken to you that My joy may remain in you, and that your joy may be full. This is My commandment, that you love one another as I have loved you. Greater love has no one than this, than to lay down one's life for his friends. You are My friends if you do whatever I command you. No longer do I call you servants, for a servant does not know what his master is doing; but I have called you friends, for all things that I heard from My Father I have made known to you. You did not choose Me, but I chose you and appointed you that you should go and bear fruit, and that your fruit should remain, that whatever you ask the Father in My name He may give you. These things I have commanded you, that you love one another. If the world hates you, you know that it hated Me before it hated you. If you were of the world, the world would love its own. Yet because you are not of the world, but I choose you out of the world, therefore the world hates you.

As the Father felt and acted as God Himself does toward Me, I also have felt and acted as God Himself does toward you; abide in My love. If you keep My commandments, you will abide in My love, just as I have kept My Father's commandments and abide in His love. These things I have spoken to you that My joy may remain in you, and that your joy may be full. This is My commandment, that you feel and act as God Himself does toward one another as I have felt and acted as God Himself did toward you. Greater love has no one than this, than to lay down one's life for his friends. You are My friends if you do whatever I command you. No longer do I call you servants, for a servant does not know what his master is doing; but I have called you friends, for all things that I heard from My Father I have made known to you. You did not choose Me, but I chose you and appointed you that you should go and bear fruit, and that your fruit should remain, that whatever you ask the Father in My name He may give you. These things I have commanded you, that you feel and act as God Himself does toward one another. If the world feels and acts the opposite way that God Himself does towards you, you know that it felt and acted the opposite way that God Himself did toward Me before it felt and acted the opposite way that God Himself did toward you. If you were of the world, the world would feel and act as God Himself does toward its own. Yet because you are not of the world, but I choose you out of the world, therefore the world feels and acts the opposite way that God Himself does towards you.

18. By this we know love, because He laid down His life for us. And we also ought to lay down our life for the brethren. But whoever has this world's goods, and sees his brother in need, and shuts up his heart from him, how does the love of God abide in him?

By this we know God, because He laid down His life for us. And we also ought to lay down our life for the brethren. But whoever has this world's goods, and sees his brother in need, and shuts up his heart from him, how does God abide in him?

19. Beloved, let us love one another, for love is of God; and everyone who loves is born of God and knows God. He who does not love does not know God, for GOD IS LOVE. In this the love of God was manifest toward us—that God has sent His only begotten Son into the world, that we may live through Him. In this is love, not that we loved God, but that He loved us and sent His Son to be the propitiation for our sins. Beloved, if God so loves us, we also ought to love one another. No one has seen God at any time. If we love one another, God abides in us, and His love has been perfected in us. By this we know that we abide in Him, and He in us, because He has given us His Spirit. And we have seen and testify that the Father has sent the Son as Savior of the world.

Whoever confesses that Jesus is the Son of God, God abides in him, and he in God. And we have known and believed the love that God has for us. God is love, and he who abides in love abides in God, and God in him. Love has been perfected among us in this: that we may have boldness in the day of judgment; because as He is, so are we in the world. There is no fear in love; but perfect love casts out fear, because fear involves torment. But he who fears has not been made perfect in love.

We love Him because He first loved us. If someone says, "I love God," and then hates his brother, he is a liar, for he who does not love his brother who he has seen, how can he love God whom he has not seen? Whoever believes that Jesus the Christ is born of God, and everyone who loves Him who begot loves Him who is begotten of Him. By this we know that we are the children of God, when we love God and keep His commandments. For this is the love of God, that we keep His commandments. And His commandments are not burdensome, For whatever is born of God overcomes the world. And this is the victory that has overcome the world—our faith. Who is he that overcomes the world but he who believes that Jesus is the Son of God?

Beloved, let us feel and act as God Himself does toward one another, for God is of God; and everyone who feels and acts as God Himself does towards another is born of God and knows God. He who does not feel and act as God Himself does toward others does not know God, for GOD IS God. In this the feelings and actions of God Himself toward us was manifest to us—that God has sent His only begotten Son into the world, that we may live through Him. In this is God, not that we felt and acted as God Himself did toward God, but that He felt and acted as God Himself did toward us and sent His Son to be the propitiation for our sins. Beloved, if God so loves us, we also ought to feel and act as God Himself does toward one another. No one has seen God at any time. If we feel and act as God Himself does toward one another, God abides in us, and the feelings and actions of God Himself toward others has been perfected in us. By this we know that we abide in Him, and He in us, because He has given us His Spirit. And we have seen and testify that the Father has sent the Son as Savior of the world.

Whoever confesses that Jesus is the Son of God, God abides in him, and he in God. And we have known and believed the feelings and actions of God Himself toward us that God has for us. God is God, and he who abides in God abides in God, and God in him. God has been perfected among us in this: that we may have boldness in the day of judgment; because as He is, so are we in the world. There is no fear in God; but God casts out fear, because fear involves torment. But he who fears has not been made perfect in God.

We feel and act as God Himself does toward Him because He first felt and acted as God Himself did toward us. If someone says, "I feel and act as God Himself does toward God," and then hates his brother, he is a liar, for he who does not feel and act as God Himself does toward his brother whom he has seen, how can he feel and act as God Himself does toward God whom he has not seen? Whoever believes that Jesus is the Christ is born of God, and everyone who feels and acts as God Himself does towards Him who begot feels and acts as God Himself does towards Him who is begotten of Him. By this we know that we are the children of God, when we feel and act as God Himself does toward God and keep His commandments. For this is the love of God, that we keep His commandments. And His commandments are not burdensome, For whatever is born of God overcomes the world. And this is the victory that has overcome the world—our faith. Who is he that overcomes the world but he who believes that Jesus is the Son of God?

LOVE IS THE ANSWER!

GOD IS THE ANSWER!

Appendix: PENIEL'S ODE

I have met Love.

Love spoke to me in His own voice and I melted with desire for Him.

I saw Love as He truly is, and were He not veiled, I would surely have perished from this mortal life.

The Love within me, which gives me life and person, sighed and communed with Love and I experienced Love as He truly is.

I was deeply changed and shall never again be the same as before.

Love gave me new eyes with which to see Him in His many disguises and veils throughout our mortal life, and now I see Him everywhere in all things.

I would willingly suffer anything if I could but gaze upon Him forevermore, unveiled and in His full glory—this is the end of my quest.

For I know to behold the true beauty of Love is to become one with Him, and I desire to be in full mystical union with Him more than all things, although I could never be worthy of such a prize.

Oh Love, my true beloved, now veiled in so many disguises, come unto me and change me into what You desire of me; I give my all to You!

Let us be one together. Let us walk Your sunny fields of cool green grass and lie in Your secret garden so that You may tell me Your secrets of Love.

Let me give You Your own sweet flowers for Your kisses.

Let us walk among Your mountains and speak with brother eagle, and then we will soar among the clouds with him.

Let us explore all of Your mystical wonderland of boundless Love and taste of all Your delights.

And when we have seen all of Your treasures, let us embrace in the heat of our mutual passion and melt together into one soul so that mine will be Yours and Yours mine.

Oh Love, why do You torture me so sweetly and hide Your face from me?

You say that I would perish from this life if I were to see You as You truly are. Well then, let me perish, for nothing is too great a price to pay to see Thee as I did before.

I am so weary of this chase, and I will always continue seeking and pursuing You until I catch You.

You have let me taste of Your sweet nectar and I burn with agony for its unforgettable fragrance and savor.

You won't let me catch You just yet.

You have tantalized me with Your mystical charm; I am Your captive and willing courtier.

Let me come and love You!

Since You will not let me catch You for now, speak to me in that beckoning voice and tell me of Yourself.

Oh, I know that You desire for me to catch You and love You; yet the chase is sweet too!

I burn with the wine of Your intoxicating desires and delights.

All along my weary path You leave me gifts of Love; hints to Your whereabouts, encouraging me to continue.

Run on my Love, for I have Your scent, and I know well Your tracks.

I can detect the scent of pomegranates in Your hair. And when brother Death finally comes out to embrace me, there You will stand on the other side awaiting my crossing so that we can embrace as One Person for all eternity.

I trust You when You tell me that I should tarry in this mortal life a little longer, as I may help some struggling pilgrims searching for the path You have shown me.

I shall wait here patiently, looking for You in all things, and following Your footsteps. If You send other travelers my way, and they are sincere, I shall tell them of You and Your Love.

Yes my friends, my love is Love—the Alpha and Omega, the Provider and Gift-giver, the Perfect Loving Father! He is our Source and our Goal, our sign and our path. Please walk with me along this mortal path seeking Truth and Perfection if you will.

My mission in life is to assist others to find The Truth, as it has been revealed to me, if they wish to learn it and remain sincere.

Please allow me the pleasure and fulfillment of assisting you to find the answers to all of the relevant questions you have.

I Love you, dear reader, and sincerely wish you success, well-being, and good fortune. May Dad show you kindness and put you in His favor eternally.

Yours In Christ,
Peniel G.G.G.

About The Author

My pen name is Peniel G.G.G. and my legal name is Mark Anthony Johnson. My current address is:

Peniel G.G.G.
P. O. Box 5182
Shawnee, OK 74804

Phone: 405-964-6436
Toll free: 1-866-MCWJ 777

Website: www.mcwj.com

My mission in life is to assist others to find the truth, if they are sincerely searching for it. Since you are reading this book, perhaps you are looking for the important truths in life. I am sure that this book can assist you. I hope that it is both entertaining and informative. Thank you for reading it.

Many of the people who know me think that I am a bit strange because I claim to have had casual conversations with Jesus. I believe that, although most of those who know me think me rather odd, they see me as a friend and a good person.

I'll admit right along with you that it seems rather extraordinary for someone to claim that he casually spoke with Jesus on a regular basis; I am very skeptical of things such as this myself. However, it was not my doing—it was His. He chose me to speak with for one simple reason: I was willing to listen. I was also committed to the truth; that is, I was willing to take what I learned and apply it in my life. I was very skeptical at first, but I did keep an open mind—as I hope you will also.

I do not offer any justification for my beliefs—this book speaks for itself. If what is said herein is good, true, or helpful to you in some way, then I have done what I intended, and it really doesn't matter if I got the information from God, my imagination, or some Cosmic Space-Surfer. *What is good is good and should be used as best it can.* Jesus has often illustrated this point to me, and I would feel contemptuous doubting the reasonableness of such wisdom. All that I ask of you is that you read my book with an open mind. I am sure that you will base your opinions concerning it on the reasonableness of the wisdom contained therein. I ask nothing else of you here.

Jesus and I started talking in 1979; the subjects covered just about everything you could imagine. This particular book was written in 1985.

Much of what is contained in these written conversations we had covered years before, yet we wished to recapture the initial mood of the talk. I admit that some of it was a little "staged" and with the intention of assisting the reader to more easily grasp what is being said.

I make no apology for these conversations. They are beautiful and helpful to those searching for truth, those whose soil is properly prepared.

I love you, dear reader, even if I do not yet know you! I hope to know you someday if that is your wish. I have many things to tell you that are wonderful and beautiful (if you'll give me the chance!).

Throughout this book I make extensive use of **boldface** and underlining to emphasize or stress speech nuances that cannot adequately be shown on paper. For clarity, Jesus' words will be shown in a different font than mine.

I often refer to the male gender when speaking in general terms. Please take such usage of the male gender with a grain of salt, for I usually mean to refer to all people, not just we vain and self-centered men.

May Dad put you eternally in His favor and give you True Peace.

Friend,

CONTACT ME!

I can help.

www.mcwj.com

or call

Peniel G.G.G.

405-964-6436

Toll free: 1-866-MCWJ 777

Printed in the United States
1093000002B/292-390

9 780958 054379